The Heart and Mind in Teaching

Other Books By the Authors

Consensus: Education Reform Is Possible by William Hayes

What's Ahead in Education?: An Analysis of the Policies of the Obama Administration by William Hayes and John A. Martin

All New Real-Life Case Studies for Teachers by William Hayes

No Child Left Behind: Past, Present, and Future by William Hayes

All New Real-Life Case Studies for School Administrators by William Hayes

The Progressive Education Movement: Is It Still a Factor in Today's Schools? by William Hayes

Horace Mann's Vision of the Public Schools: Is it Still Relevant? by William Hayes

Are We Still a Nation at Risk Two Decades Later? by William Hayes

So You Want to Be a Principal? by William Hayes

So You Want to Be a College Professor? by William Hayes

So You Want to Be a Superintendent? by William Hayes

Real-Life Case Studies for School Board Members by William Hayes

So You Want to Be a School Board Member? by William Hayes

Real-Life Case Studies for School Administrators by William Hayes

Real-Life Case Studies for Teachers by William Hayes

The Heart and Mind in Teaching

Pedagogical Styles through the Ages

Alyssa Magee Lowery and William Hayes

ROWMAN & LITTLEFIELD
Lanham • Boulder • New York • London

KH

Published by Rowman & Littlefield
A wholly owned subsidiary of The Rowman & Littlefield Publishing Group, Inc.
4501 Forbes Boulevard, Suite 200, Lanham, Maryland 20706
www.rowman.com

16 Carlisle Street, London W1D 3BT, United Kingdom

British Library Cataloguing in Publication Information Available

Library of Congress Cataloging-in-Publication Data Available

978-1-4758-0543-7 (cloth : alk. paper)
978-1-4758-0544-4 (pbk. : alk. paper)
978-1-4758-0545-1 (electronic)

♾ ™ The paper used in this publication meets the minimum requirements of American National Standard for Information Sciences Permanence of Paper for Printed Library Materials, ANSI/NISO Z39.48-1992.

Printed in the United States of America

12/17/15

Teaching is the most difficult of all arts, and the profoundest of all sciences. . . . Arithmetic, grammar, and the other rudiments, as they are called, comprise but a small part of the teachings in a school. The rudiments of feeling are taught not less than the rudiments of thinking.
—Horace Mann, *First Annual Report of the Secretary of the Massachusetts Board of Education*

Contents

Acknowledgments

We would first like to thank our Roberts Wesleyan colleagues Linda Jones and Marty Garland, who helped with the proofreading and research for this project. In addition, we are grateful to Tom Koerner, our editor, for his support and assistance in the preparation of the book. Alyssa wishes to thank her husband, Joshua, for his patience and willingness to proof-listen. She would also like to thank her parents, who have always been number one fans of her work, and Mr. Hayes, who presented her with the wonderful opportunity to contribute to this book. Finally, Bill is indebted to his wife, Nancy, who has been an essential supporter and proofreader in all of his sixteen books.

Foreword

Across the nation, in thousands of communities large and small, there is an overwhelming consensus about the importance of education for individual development, for economic growth, and for civic health. Equally impressive are the deep divides about the best strategies to achieve educational success. Educational reforms are continuous, divisive, and often nonproductive. Colleges and universities with programs to prepare teachers are also pulled in different directions and have come under heightened scrutiny. The stakes are enormous, and the vested interests are impassioned.

If matters of religion and politics are not to be discussed in polite company, perhaps the topic of educational reform should be added to that list because the differences are so profound and the search for common ground so rare. Meanwhile, scholars, publishers, and political advocates continue to fill our libraries and airwaves with the latest opinions, recommendations, and data.

In the midst of these pundit proclamations, my colleague Professor Bill Hayes and his coauthor Alyssa Magee Lowery offer an important contribution to our historical and contemporary understanding of teaching pedagogy. Professor Hayes has distinguished himself as an effective teacher at both the high school and the college level, and he has provided effective educational leadership during a long career as principal and superintendent in western New York. In addition, he is a prolific author, providing keen historical insights and commonsense advice about such educational reforms as No Child Left Behind.

His coauthor for this book is Alyssa Magee Lowery, a 2012 honors graduate of Roberts Wesleyan College. While she continues her career as an elementary teacher, she will be seeking a graduate degree in the field of English. Those who know her are convinced that she is destined for a successful career both as an author and as a professor of English.

Recognizing that what counts in educational effectiveness is the relationship between student and teacher, Hayes and Lowery help us to look afresh at the practice of good teaching, focusing in the end on whether good teaching is science or art. Their historical analysis is enlightening, and their appeals to see the art of good teaching are compelling. While not demonizing the science of teaching, they demonstrate how a scientific approach will not, by itself, produce educated students, professionals, or citizens. This is an essential reminder to educational reformers, politicians, and parents, as well as to the teachers themselves.

In my own role as a college chief academic officer for more than twenty-five years, I have hired, mentored, and evaluated hundreds of faculty members. Some teachers just do not get it; many teachers work hard and effectively; and a few teachers are truly superb. In my view, what characterizes the latter two groups and what distinguishes the few is their understanding that effective teaching is both art and science, not one or the other. We know a lot more about how students learn and about how pedagogy affects that learning through the science of education, and the best teachers are those who continue to learn about learning. We also know that the best teachers are those who love their students and their disciplines and have the freedom and the desire to be creative, passionate, and relational. Science cannot teach us to love or create, but it can help us, in part, to understand whether our love and creativity are having an impact on student learning.

We all remember teachers who made a difference, who lit fires in our minds and shaped our characters. The best teaching is neither pure art nor pure science but, rather, the explosive mixture that produces richly informed and deeply committed artists, scientists, and citizens. Our future, both as individuals and as communities, depends on the effectiveness of our educational efforts.

Dr. Robert Zwier
Provost of Roberts Wesleyan College

Introduction

Webster's New World Dictionary includes in the definitions of the words *teach* and *teaching* such phrases as "showing how to do something; training . . . to give lessons; instruct; to provide with knowledge and insight." With these definitions, it is undoubtedly true that teaching has been an essential part of life on this earth for a very long time. The purpose of this book is not to write a complete history of the teaching process. What is attempted here is to identify and describe various individuals and historical movements that have influenced the evolution of teaching in the United States.

Our story begins with a select discussion of European individuals and historic movements that have had a significant impact on teaching in the United States. We begin with the study of education in ancient Greece, then jump ahead centuries and focus on the teaching methods used in the spread of Christianity. The final stop on this brief survey of teaching prior to the colonization of North America is a consideration of the European Renaissance and its effect on the way that students are taught.

With the age of colonization, the next emphasis is placed on the early education system in the United States. This includes a discussion of the common school movement and the contributions of Horace Mann. The influence of progressivism features the impact of John Dewey and Maria Montessori. Jumping to the twentieth century, we then consider the lesson-planning process advocated by Madeline Hunter. As the federal government entered the education field with the Individuals with Disabilities Education Act and No Child Left Behind, what occurred in schools would be greatly affected. As a result, these crucial developments in our country's education system deserve careful consideration.

The final aspect of the book is devoted to current trends, and the focus is the impact of the Common Core curriculum and the changes being brought about by educational technology. Throughout the text, we consider the age-old question of whether teaching is primarily an art or a science.

There are a number of definitions of art. The first word used in the definition in *Webster's New World Dictionary* is "creativeness." Another definition, given by Google, defines art as "the expression or application of human creative skill and imagination." As for science, the first word used by *Webster's* is "systematized." Google defines science as "the intellectual and practical activity encompassing the systematic study of the

structure and behavior of the physical and natural." Based on these definitions, an exploration of this essential question of teaching as an art or a
science, combined with an in-depth look at the history of pedagogy, will
undoubtedly lead us to a fuller, richer understanding and appreciation of
the remarkable profession that is teaching.

I

Past

ONE

Teaching in Antiquity

The history of teaching dates back hundreds of thousands of years, and quite frankly, it would be rather impossible to start at the very beginning. In the interest of brevity, it seems fitting to begin with the contribution of one civilization that asked the very same question that we are wrestling with today: What are the necessary components of good teaching? We begin with a brief overview of the educational climate in ancient Greece, move onto analyses of Greece's major educational theorists and their contributions to the modern teaching profession, and then trace the migration of their ideals to Rome, the civilization that spread throughout the then-known world.

The fifth century BC was a time of tumult for Greece, bringing a clash between the old and the new. For years, schooling had been designed by individual city-states, resulting in a variety of educational focuses and outcomes. However, the eventual demise of each city-state's way of educating its youth gave way to a "new" Greece that produced some of the first educational theorists.

In famed militaristic Sparta, teachers were mentors who taught seven- to eighteen-year-old young men how to be loyal citizens and how to prepare for their upcoming careers as warriors.[1] Young girls were taught to cast aside delicacy and to focus on becoming strong childbearers, even appearing naked at feasts to squelch romantic notions of mating and to embrace their true purposes, which were to produce fine young soldiers.[2]

Although Sparta had flourished as one of Greece's most successful city-states for a century, its development seemed to freeze around 550 bc, when a political and social revolution took hold and elevated the aristocracy to impossible heights. The retaliation of the people took precedence over physicality and art, areas that were viewed to produce strong personalities. As a result, according to one expert, "Spartan education grew

petrified, exaggerating its peculiarities with an increasing despairing vio-
lence as its sense of its own futility increased."[3]

Meanwhile, in Athens, young men enjoyed private state-provided educations from sixteen to twenty years of age that trained them not only
for military careers but in the humanities, science, and gymnastics.[4] Plato
described Athenian education as "two-sided," partly gymnastics for the
body and partly music for the soul. It should be understood that the term
gymnastics refers to physical education in general and that *music* includes
all artistic pursuits.[5]

This Athenian idea of educating men who were both artistic and athletic began to give way to a new theory of education, led by innovators
whom we now call *Sophists*. Greek society was facing a fairly major problem. The men who were coming into political and artistic prominence
had the equivalents of elementary school educations. Although the initial
response was to develop schools of medicine and philosophy, these systems did not gain a foothold in Greek society.[6]

Rather, the Sophists observed the active democracy in Athens and
sought to produce educated and capable statesmen. Therefore, sophistry
had a far more technical emphasis, effectively widening the scope of
Greek education. The history of modern teaching begins here.

The swing away from old Greek education brought the first focus on
teaching as a profession. In fact, when asked to define his art, one the first
Sophists, Protagoras, called it "the education of men."[7] Although sophistry had overarching themes, content was not common among its practitioners. Rather, the common thread among Sophists was simply the fact
that they were educators.

They did not open any schools, but they did engage in large-scale
tutoring. Taking on groups of young men under contracts for three to
four years of education, they were the first to ask for payment. As a
result, they had to actively seek students and advertise themselves in
different towns using free sample lectures and debates. Today's public
lectures can be directly traced to the activity of the early Sophists.[8]

Sophist lectures were similar to our own world of advertisement in
that they often contained some element of "razzle-dazzle." Sophists did
not shy away from claiming to know everything, often speaking from a
throne high in the air and wearing regal purple robes. Young men were
drawn to their mystique and apparent great knowledge, rarely hesitating
to join them.[9]

As to the nature of Sophist education, it was the intention of these
teachers to train excellent politicians, and the previous attention given to
speculation about the nature of life and the gods was considered useless.
Protagoras mused, "I do not know whether they [the gods] exist or not. It
is a difficult question, and life is too short." What the Sophists regarded
as worthy of study was political life and *hic et nunc*, or the ability to make
an audience admit the probability of anything.

One of the few epithets passed down from Protagoras, "Man is the measure of all things," eloquently summarizes the intention of Sophist education, which truly was a sort of relativism. According to a historian of the period, "They never taught their pupils any truth about being or man, but merely how to be always, and in any kind of circumstances, right." [10]

Of course, this is not the direction that education would continue to take. The decline of sophistry came rather quickly, although its impact on the future of teaching remains evident in the continued existence of higher education and teaching as a profession. A new generation of Greek educators shifted educational theory, subtly at first, ultimately arriving at a new school almost wholly unrecognizable as an offshoot of sophistry.

The change began with Socrates, who was essentially the bridge between sophistry and classical Greek education. He was the first to verbally state the conflict between the old and new schools of thought about education and to suggest a vague solution. Although he accepted Protagoras's assertion that "man is the measure of all things," he added the claim that would shape new educational theory: man must know himself. The addition of such a revolutionary idea shifted the Sophist view that knowledge could be manipulated on the basis of opinion. Instead, the universality of knowledge was recognized, giving way to Socrates's "Knowledge is virtue" principle. [11]

The implications for teaching were incredible. With a new perception of knowledge as a universal entity came the potential for teaching processes and theories. Of particular interest is the Socratic method, a process of induction for arriving at a logical conclusion through discussion. It should be noted that the Socratic method does not have the logical conclusion as its ultimate goal but the strengthening of the mind in the process.

Even though we regard Socrates's contributions as valuable and significant, they brought about his historical destruction. In 399 BC, he was accused of heresy and corruption of the youth and did nothing to help his defense when he accused the jury of thinking illogically, implying that he ought to be thanked rather than persecuted. He was sentenced to death and drank his cup of poison hemlock reservedly while he engaged in final dialogues with his friends and students. [12]

Socrates's legacy is an impressive one. The teaching profession has him to thank for many of its foundational principles, including the value of knowledge, discussion as a means for uncovering objective knowledge, and the development of critical thinking skills. His effects did not end there, though. Among his many students is one historical figure who would continue to improve on the theories of his mentor.

Plato was despondent after the execution of his mentor, and he joined a group of his fellow disciples in exile at Megara, rejecting the society that had convicted his beloved teacher. Upon his return to Athens, he opened his famed Academy, where he lectured without manuscript and developed a specific method for teaching.[13]

Described in detail in his *Dialogue*, his form should sound familiar to most who have studied educational theory. A question is put forward and discussed by the group. Through the discussion, a counterargument is developed and discussed, allowing the teacher to guide students toward a conclusion.[14] Because Plato believed that nothing can be known with complete objectivity, this dialogue demonstrated to students that only through discussion and exploration can we shape definitions.

Coming down decidedly on the science end of the great science/humanities debate (one seen in both Hellenistic and modern society), Plato developed the first notion that philosophical, social, and political realities were affected by scientific fact.[15] The existence of secondary schools with integrated curriculum and permanent specialized instructors can also be attributed to Plato, who essentially invented the university with his Academy.[16]

We also owe the concept of "education for everyone" to Plato. An early defender of education for women, he argued that the purpose of education was twofold: to determine aptitude and to provide career preparation. As such, he elected to offer a liberal education to his students. Ideally, Plato asserted that students should study gymnastics and music during childhood, scientific higher education from twenty to thirty, and philosophical education for five years after that.[17] Such a system is remarkably similar to the system of high school, undergraduate, and advanced degree tracks that are in place today.

Following the train of educational theorists, we arrive next at a disciple of Plato. Aristotle's influence on the modern teaching profession is considered by some to be greater than that of any other Greek educational theorist. His major contributions include peripatetic teaching and the systemization of knowledge. The term *peripatetic* came from the tendency of masters and students to continue their discussions while walking. At his school, the Lyceum, Aristotle offered morning advanced lectures for his students and afternoon talks for the general public.[18]

More important, he introduced scientific method to his students, emphasizing detailed study and adding deductive reasoning to Socrates's method of inductive reasoning. With writings about such subjects as "anatomy, astronomy, botany, ethics, history, literary criticism, logic, mathematics, metaphysics, rhetoric, philosophy, physics, psychology, and zoology," his reach was vast, resulting in the greatest attempt in antiquity to gather and evaluate knowledge.[19] In fact, the Lyceum was widely known for its large staff of workers, an enormous library, and large collection of museum specimens and maps.[20]

Here we see an obvious shift from the previous focus on moral and philosophical well-being. This focus on scholasticism would serve as the basis of institutionalized education in the Middle Ages.[21] It has been suggested,

> Aristotle is the first giant orderer of the universe of thought. . . . For it is no exaggeration to say that he laid the basis of our scholarly vocabulary in the whole broad field of the humanities, and that from his work issued the development of the higher curriculum. . . . Even the essential categories of natural philosophy have sprung from his mind.[22]

Furthermore, Aristotle presented the first idea of a common core of knowledge that was basic to education, including reading, writing, music, and physical education. Such a concept is clearly mirrored in American school systems today.[23]

Educational theory, though a common topic for today's students and professors, was born of the Greek theorists. Even the concept of this book, which looks at the evolution of teaching, is owed to the brilliant men who first considered what it means to know and how teachers can expedite the learning. Metacognition, or thinking about thought, was not a part of society before the arrival of great thinkers such as the Sophists, Socrates, Plato, and Aristotle. Both the institutions of learning that we know today and the teaching methods that we employ echo those developed in ancient Greece.

To trace the path of Hellenistic wisdom to the present, we must examine Rome, the bridge between the era of Greek philosophy and the universities of the Middle Ages. With the translation of Homer's *Odyssey* into Latin came a flood of Hellenistic wisdom into the previously simple Roman school system. From 776 BC to about 250 BC, Roman children had mainly been educated in the home, where they studied the traditions of the state and memorized the Law of the Twelve Tables, the basic tenets to which Roman citizens were expected to adhere.[24] Elementary schools called *ludi* provided the only formal education available and gave instruction only in reading and writing.[25]

Following the translation of the *Odyssey* by Livius Andronicus, there was a rapid increase in the literary content available in Roman schools. More and more Greek works became available in the ludi, effectively transforming them from rudimentary schools to schools of grammar and rhetoric.[26] By 50 AD, Roman education was considered "Hellenized," and it resembled the schools of Athens much more closely than the basic ludi of Rome's past.

A Roman child would attend a "school of the literator" at a young age and study under a *ludimagister*. This education included basic reading, writing, and calculation and served as a precursor to the "school of the Grammaticus," to which a student could transfer after demonstrating the ability to read ordinary prose. Grammar schools were more formal in terms of method, curriculum, and public support, and they fell into two categories: Greek and Latin. The latter would come into greater prominence than the former, lasting until the decline of Rome, around 200 AD.[27]

The Latin grammar school—more commonly known as a *literatus* or *Grammaticus*—included study of linguistics and literary criticism of history, science, and poetry as well as mathematics, music, and dialectics, but unlike the Greek schools, it neglected gymnastics and dance. Such a curriculum might remind one of the studies offered in twenty-first-century high schools. Students were also trained in declamation, a combination of grammar and rhetoric, which was viewed as the culmination of a practical literary education.[28]

Again, as in modern American education, students who finished Latin grammar school might go on to university. Roman libraries and universities were highly similar to Greek universities and libraries, largely because libraries were taken as spoils of war in Roman conquests of Greece. The famous University of Rome, later called the *Athenaeum*, originated in the library founded by Vespasian and subsidized by Hadrian. Much like modern college students, students who studied in Roman universities studied more specialized areas, such as medicine and law.[29]

Even though Greek educators provided the basis for the educational system in Rome, it is the Roman style of education that became more influential to the modern world. In fact, Cicero's *Institutes of Oratory* was rediscovered and translated in 1411 and used by humanistic educational theorists as the basis of their teachings.[30] In his twelve-book composition, Cicero made many assertions that would not seem out of place in a modern education textbook.

One such assertion is his reference to the individual differences among students, stating that although students possess different areas of strength, most are capable of improvement. He also recognized public education as a more beneficial situation than a home-based private education because it afforded students the opportunity to learn from one another as well as from a teacher. He also filled eleven books with descriptions of advanced education programs designed to fulfill civic needs, similar to today's trade schools and schools of professional education.[31] His advocacy for broad general education as the basis of success and his early conception of the "humanities" as an area of study make Cicero one of the real fathers of modern education.

One great educational question that was not answered by the theorists of Greco-Roman education is still in play today. Is teaching an art or a science? Note that when Protagoras the Sophist was asked to define his art, he answered, "The education of men." Even Socrates, often mocked for his eccentric behavior, seemed to approach teaching with more of an artistic flair:

> He walked about Athens barefooted, in a coarse cheap robe, talking incessantly and gathering people about him. Sometimes he would go

into a trance; then, rapt in thought, he would stand for hours, even for an entire night, unconscious of what was going on about him. . . . The comedy writers of his age ridiculed and satirized him on the stage. He is depicted by one author in his "thinking shop" studying astronomy from a basket suspended in mid-air and uttering nonsense to interested students.[32]

Socrates's less systemized process stands in sharp contrast to that of his philosophical descendents, especially to that of Aristotle, with his emphasis on objectivity and detailed study of the seen. Roman emphasis on the arts of rhetoric and oratory presents a stark difference from the studies of law and medicine emphasized in the Roman *Athenaeum*.

A study of Greco-Roman educational theory offers no definitive answers into the art/science debate in education, but it does provide us with a starting point from which to trace our lineage as educators. In the next chapter, we consider particularly artistic teachers who did not theorize about education but instead put great teaching into practice.

NOTES

1. Francesco Cordasco, *A Brief History of Education* (Totowa, NJ: Littlefield, Adams, 1970), 4–7.

2. H. I. Marrou, *A History of Education in Antiquity* (New York: Sheed & Ward, 1956), 23.

3. Marrou, *A History of Education in Antiquity*, 19.

4. Cordasco, *A Brief History of Education*, 4–7.

5. Marrou, *A History of Education in Antiquity*, 41.

6. Marrou, *A History of Education in Antiquity*, 46–47.

7. Marrou, *A History of Education in Antiquity*, 49.

8. Marrou, *A History of Education in Antiquity*, 51.

9. Marrou, *A History of Education in Antiquity*, 50.

10. Marrou, *A History of Education in Antiquity*, 50.

11. Cordasco, *A Brief History of Education*, 7.

12. Franklin J. Meine and Harris Gaylord Warren, eds., "Socrates," in *Great Leaders: Men and Women Who Influenced Their Times* (Chicago: University of Knowledge, 1938), 346.

13. Meine and Warren, "Plato," in *Great Leaders*, 307–8.

14. Meine and Warren, "Plato," in *Great Leaders*, 307–8.

15. Frederick A. G. Beck, *Greek Education: 450–350 BC* (New York: Barnes & Noble, 1964), 240.

16. Beck, *Greek Education*, 240.

17. Cordasco, *A Brief History of Education*, 7.

18. Meine and Warren, "Aristotle," in *Great Leaders*, 26–28.

19. Meine and Warren, "Aristotle," in *Great Leaders*, 26–28.

20. Meine and Warren, "Aristotle," in *Great Leaders*, 26–28.

21. Cordasco, *A Brief History of Education*, 8–9.

22. Robert Ulich, "Aristotle," in *Three Thousand Years of Educational Wisdom: Selections from Great Document* (Cambridge, MA: Harvard University Press, 1971), 62.

23. L. Dean Webb, Arlene Metha, and K. Forbis Jordan, "American Education: European Heritage and Colonial Experience," in *Foundations of American Education* (Upper Saddle River, NJ: Prentice Hall, 2000), 135.

24. Edward D. Myers, *Education in the Perspective of History* (New York: Harper & Brothers, 1960), 107.

25. Cordasco, *A Brief History of Education*, 13–14.

26. Cordasco, *A Brief History of Education*, 14.

27. Cordasco, *A Brief History of Education*, 15.

28. Cordasco, *A Brief History of Education*, 15.

29. Cordasco, *A Brief History of Education*, 16.

30. Cordasco, *A Brief History of Education*, 17–18.

31. Cordasco, *A Brief History of Education*, 17–18.

32. Meine and Warren, "Plato," in *Great Leaders*, 344.

TWO

Teaching Methods in Early Christianity

Given his lasting success as a teacher, there is surprisingly little scholarship on the teaching style of Jesus of Nazareth. The mere fact that millions of people around the world still regard themselves as his disciples speaks to his influence, and such a teacher merits close study by any person interested in the craft. Although many would quarrel with his content, there can be little argument that he was an effective teacher, and for that reason, we look solely at his delivery and refrain from commenting on his claims.

Even though only three years of his life were dedicated to active teaching, it would be false to assume that Jesus showed no aptitude or interest in teaching for the first thirty years of his life. In fact, the gospel of Luke tells the story of twelve-year-old Jesus's parents in a frantic search for him after leaving the Feast of the Passover in Jerusalem. "After three days they found him in the temple courts, sitting among the teachers, listening to them and asking them questions. Everyone who heard him was amazed at his understanding and his answers." [1]

Jesus would become a radical teacher, but on the surface, his methods bore significant resemblance to those of his contemporaries. Jesus gathered disciples who traveled with him, learning his philosophy and assisting him in his teaching. [2] Together, they traveled throughout southeast Galilee and Jerusalem, teaching not only at their chosen destinations but on route to those locations. [3] Acclaimed historian Paul Johnson says, "There is no evidence he preached formal sermons, let alone regular, repeated ones. Indeed, the word 'preached' should not be used about him. 'Taught' is more accurate." [4]

The difference between the two is critical and is the starting point for a real analysis of Jesus's teaching. Rather than limiting his teaching to lectures, Jesus taught through words and deeds.[5] His messages permeated not only his verbal teachings but his demeanor and actions: "Love the Lord your God with all your heart and with all your soul and with all your mind and with all your strength" and "Love your neighbor as yourself." Historic accounts by his disciples show him bestowing previously unheard-of equal status on children;[6] showing respect and kindness to women, who at the time were considered little more than property;[7] and interacting fearlessly and kindly with lepers, even extending a hand to touch them.[8]

In an infographic called "Smart Teaching: Understanding What a Brain Can't Ignore," created by Chris Lema, there is a section called "The ABC's of Sticky Teaching."[9] Here, Lema highlights good teaching practice, supporting his assertions with examples of Jesus's teaching:

- Awaken the intrigue
- Begin and end often
- Create contrast
- Draw them in with stories
- Emotion drives attention
- Focus on the big idea

"Awaken the intrigue" is something of which Jesus was a master. He knew exactly how to be ambiguous at the right times, drawing the interest of those around him. In the gospel of Matthew, the following account is given of the calling of the first disciples: "They were casting a net into the lake, for they were fisherman. 'Come, follow me,' Jesus said, 'and I will make you fishers of men.' At once they left their nets and followed him."[10] Such an unusual request undoubtedly drew the interest of Peter and Andrew, and they responded favorably.

According to Lema's infographic, "interrupts make the brain check in." For this reason, beginning and ending instruction often gives the brain a chance to refresh itself.[11] A quick perusal of the gospel of Mark finds such phrases as "They went across the lake to the region of the Garasenes,"[12] "When Jesus had again crossed over by boat to the other side of the lake,"[13] "Jesus left there and went to his hometown,"[14] and "Then Jesus went around teaching from village to village."[15]

There is a reason that Jesus did not set up camp in one temple and teach there constantly. Instead, he traveled to new places with his disciples, using teachable moments and moving along quickly instead of using previously written sermons and delivering them from a pulpit. Not only did this guarantee that his teaching would reach a wider audience, but it helped his disciples improve their learning through the creation of variety and interest.

Also contributing to the sense of interest surrounding the teachings of Jesus was the presence of contrast in his teachings. The "You have heard it said. . . . But I tell you . . . " template made frequent appearances in the teachings of Jesus of Nazareth. "You have heard that it was said to the people long ago, 'Do not murder.' . . . But I tell you that anyone who is angry with his brother will be subject to judgment."[16] Five more instances of this template occur within the fifth chapter of Matthew.

Even in his actions, Jesus created contrast. Religious leaders of Jesus's time laid a heavy emphasis on strictly following the Old Testament laws. However, Jesus and his disciples were confronted by the Pharisees for not fasting, an action that stood in stark contrast to the behaviors of other rabbis.[17] His willingness to spend time with tax collectors and "sinners" also attracted negative attention from religious leaders and created positive contrast. When others noticed his outreach, it made them ask questions, creating another opportunity for Jesus to further his message. "It is not the healthy who need a doctor, but the sick. I have not come to call the righteous, but sinners."[18]

The use of stories is one of the most easily identifiable characteristics of Jesus's teaching. When his disciples asked him why he spoke so often in parables, he replied, "The knowledge of the secrets of the kingdom of heaven has been given to you, but not to them."[19] Jesus knew that his teachings would not be easy for his listeners to grasp, so he spoke in a way that he knew they would understand. Fifty-seven parables appear in the gospels, compared to only one sermon. Lema offers a second explanation for Jesus's use of parables. "The brain is constantly trying to save your life. So everything else is competing with it. Stories build trust, which enables the brain to take a break."[20]

Although Jesus appears to have been generally mild mannered, he allowed his emotions to surface at the appropriate moments:

> Jesus entered the temple area and drove out all who were buying and selling there. He overturned the tables of the money changers and the benches of those selling doves. "It is written," he said to them, "'My house will be called a house of prayer,' but you are making it a 'den of robbers.'"

This action attracted the attention of all those in the temple. As Lema writes, "emotion drives attention," a truth that Jesus undoubtedly knew and used to his instructional advantage.

What set Jesus apart from the Pharisees, Sadducees, and other religious leaders of his time was his focus on the main idea. At a time when the law and the rules of the Jewish faith were synonymous, there were myriad rules and regulations required of the people. This reality is what prompted the Pharisees to approach Jesus with a trick question. "One of them, an expert in the law, tested him with this question: 'Teacher, which is the greatest commandment in the Law?'" Such a question was designed as a trap. In the minds of the religious leaders, it would be heresy to suggest that there was a "greatest commandment."

Jesus replied: "'Love the Lord your God with all your heart and with all your soul and with all your mind.' This is the first and greatest commandment. And the second is like it: 'Love your neighbor as your-self.' All the Law and the Prophets hang on these two command-ments."[21]

Rather than focus on individual rules in detail, Jesus allowed those com-mandments to be the focus of all his teaching. Lema suggests, "When data is stored in the brain, only the 'main thing' gets stored. Like reading headlines. So stick with the big idea and repeat it often."[22]

Jesus of Nazareth understood these educational principles and knew how to use them to his advantage. His success remains evident because millions of people are still studying his teachings. His knowledge was also passed on to his disciples, who were charged with the task of spread-ing his message after his death. Years later, one follower of Jesus contin-ued to employ good teaching methods to further the gospel.

Paul of Tarsus, or Saint Paul, was born the son of a Jewish Roman citizen and was educated in both Jewish and Roman cultures. Historians Franklin J. Meine and Harris Gaylord Warren explain, "At that time both the Roman and the Hebrew civilizations were in essence legal; the Roman was built on the law of the civil courts, stern and unrelenting, while the Hebrew, equally stern and unrelenting, was based on the writings of the Prophets." With such a background, it is hardly surprising that Paul began his career as an advocate of the legal system. It is also of little surprise that he reacted negatively to the teachings of a man who claimed to be the Messiah and who actively led people away from the law that Paul loved so dearly.[23]

Paul's mind and occupation changed abruptly when he claimed to have been struck blind on his way to Damascus and heard the words, "Paul, Paul, why do you persecute me?" The voice claimed to belong to Jesus, and it instructed Paul to go into the city and wait for instructions. After three days, a follower of Jesus named Ananias went to Paul and restored his sight. Paul stayed for several days with the disciples of Jesus in Damascus and promptly began teaching their message in the syn-agogues.[24]

His two major journeys through Syria and Asia Minor were not with-out troubles, including a two-year stint in a Roman prison and death by the sword as commanded by Nero's court.[25] Before this tragic turn, how-ever, Paul excelled as a preacher and wrote many famous letters to the churches that he planted on his journey.[26] His style, however, is notably different from the one exhibited by Jesus of Nazareth.

Paul's difference in style can be accounted for by an upbringing very different from that of Jesus of Nazareth. As a Roman citizen, Paul was likely well versed in oratorical and rhetorical theory. In fact, it is Paul who comes the closest to what would today be considered "discourse and rhetoric." An ideal example comes in Acts 17:22–31, where he speaks to the Athenians at the Areopagus:

> Paul then stood up in the meeting of the Areopagus and said: "Men of Athens! I see that in every way you are very religious. For as I walked around and looked carefully at your objects of worship, I even found an altar with this inscription: TO AN UNKNOWN GOD. Now what you worship as something unknown I am going to proclaim to you. The God who made the world and everything in it is the Lord of heaven and earth and does not live in temples built by hands. And he is not served by human hands, as if he needed anything, because he himself gives all men life and breath and everything else. From one man he made every nation of men, that they should inhabit the whole earth; and he determined the times set for them and the exact places where they should live. God did this so that men would seek him and perhaps reach out for him and find him, though he is not far from each one of us. 'For in him we live and move and have our being.' As some of your own poets have said, 'We are his offspring.' Therefore since we are God's offspring, we should not think that the divine being is like gold or silver or stone—an image made by man's design and skill. In the past God overlooked such ignorance, but now he commands all people everywhere to repent. For he has set a day when he will judge the world with justice by the man he has appointed. He has given proof of this to all men by raising him from the dead."

What we see in Paul's speech at the Areopagus is one of very few biblical examples of teaching through designed argument. He follows the rules and customs expected from speakers. F. F. Bruce, a professor of biblical criticism and exegesis, gives commentary on Paul's teaching in Athens in his *Commentary on the Book of Acts.* Referring to Paul's characterization of the Athenians as "very religious," Bruce notes that Paul is not complimenting the council. Rather, he is indicating that it is overly superstitious, a statement that follows the etiquette expected from speakers addressing the Areopagus. "We are told that it was forbidden to use complimentary exordia when addressing the Areopagus, in hope of securing its goodwill." [27]

Paul's understanding of the etiquette expected from Areopagus speakers indicates a certain level of familiarity with the scholarly community in Athens—a familiarity that sheds some light on Paul's style of exordium. Unlike Jesus of Nazareth, who relied heavily on anecdotal and relationship-based teaching techniques, Paul seems to be essentially arguing the case for Christianity to the Athenian masters of dialogue.

He even refers to the literature of the Greek poets, including Epimenides the Cretan, who wrote, "They fashioned a tomb for thee, O holy and high one— / The Cretans, always liars, evil beasts, idle bellies! / But thou art not dead; thou livest and abidest for ever; / For in thee we live and move and have our being." [28]

In his analysis of Paul's argument, Professor Bruce points out the essential piece to Paul's teaching: "The 'delicately suited allusions' to Stoic and Epicurean tenets which have been recognized in the speech, and the direct quotations from pagan poets, have their place as points of contact with the hearers, and illustrate the argument in terms familiar to them, but in no way commit the speaker to acquiescence in the realm of ideas which formed their original context."[29] Even though Paul in no way supports the beliefs and assertions of the pagan Athenians—in fact, he vehemently opposes them—he is able to use his knowledge of those beliefs to relate to the Athenians and speak a language they understood. Such a technique is akin to a modern professor drawing parallels between ancient history and current events or between a piece of literature and popular culture.

The teachings of Jesus and Paul are nearly diametrically opposite. On one hand, we see Jesus of Nazareth, who favors a more artistic style, relying on formation of relationships and appeals to human nature. On the other, Paul chooses to adopt the scientific Greco-Roman method, constructing reasoned arguments and delivering them from a lectern. They present an early example of the art/science debate that seems all the more interesting because it exists outside institutionalized education. As we continue our survey of educational history, we enter an era to which we can trace the roots of the modern university. Our next chapter discusses education in the Middle Ages and the European Renaissance, where the art/science debate first becomes a fixture in the world of education scholarship.

NOTES

1. Luke 3:46–47 (all references to the New International Version).
2. Franklin J. Meine and Harris Gaylord Warren, eds., "Jesus Christ of Nazareth," in *Great Leaders: Men and Women Who Influenced Their Times* (Chicago: University of Knowledge, 1938), 101–6.
3. Paul Johnson, *Jesus: A Biography from a Believer* (New York: Penguin Group, 2012), 81.
4. Johnson, *Jesus*, 81–82.
5. Meine and Warren, "Jesus Christ of Nazareth," 101–6.
6. Matthew 19:13–14.
7. John 4:4–26.
8. Matthew 8:1–4.
9. Chris Lema, "Smart Teaching: Understanding What the Brain Can't Ignore," 2012, https://chrislema.wpengine.com/wp-content/uploads/2012/02/stickyTmedFor Display.png.
10. Matthew 4:18–19.
11. Lema, " Smart Teaching ."
12. Mark 5:1.
13. Mark 5:21.
14. Mark 6:1.
15. Mark 6:6.

16. Matthew 5:21–22.
17. Matthew 9:14.
18. Mark 2:13–17.
19. Matthew 13:11.
20. Lema,"Smart Teaching."
21. Matthew 22:34–40.
22. Lema,"Smart Teaching."
23. Meine and Warren, "Saint Paul," in *Great Leaders*, 331–32.
24. Acts 9:1–20.
25. Meine and Warren, "Saint Paul," in *Great Leaders*, 335.
26. Meine and Warren, "Saint Paul," in *Great Leaders*, 335.
27. F. F. Bruce, *The New International Commentary on the New Testament: The Book of the Acts* (Grand Rapids, MI: Eerdmans, 1976), 355.
28. Bruce, *The New International Commentary*, 361.
29. Bruce, *The New International Commentary*, 363.

THREE

Teaching in the Middle Ages and the European Renaissance

The end of the golden educational period in Greece and Rome came abruptly. The fall of Rome brought about the end of Greco-Roman educational institutions, thereby plunging the Western world into a period of ignorance now referred to as the Dark Ages or the Middle Ages. Throughout the Middle Ages, there was a belief in Europe that privileged society was divinely divided into three classes: noblemen, who fought and governed; clerics, who led the church; and artisans, who worked with their hands. Education was designed to prepare a child for the station in life expected for his or her class rather than to expand the mind.[1] To understand how teaching has progressed, we must first examine an era during which it stalled.

For aristocratic children, some semblance of Greco-Roman education was maintained. Rudiments such as the alphabet were learned at mothers' knees, and household chaplains would provide instruction in Latin, reading, and writing. Still, for aristocratic children in the Middle Ages, manners were given greater importance than academics. According to historian Marjorie Rowling, author of *Everyday Life in Medieval Times*, "It was also necessary to become proficient at chess and backgammon, to hawk, hunt and fence, to study geometry, magic, and law."[2] Such a curriculum demonstrates a significant shift from those of the Greek and Roman empires, especially when one considers that this is the education afforded to the upper, ruling class.

Meanwhile, peasants and artisans received only enough formal education to prepare them for participation in church services. Instead of studying, they were expected to provide for their families and masters. A few particularly bright peasants were assigned to monastic schools, which provided most of the formal education in northern Europe until around 1100 AD and were able to preserve the heritage of classical learning and literature in the West, though only barely.[3] It is this presence that provided a bridge, albeit a weak one, between the golden age of classical Greco-Roman education and the next major point on the educational timeline. A small educational flame continued to burn until necessity brought about another major movement.[4]

Unfortunately, this flame was not enough to illuminate the Dark Ages. The church was distrustful of the "pagan" literary and rhetorical schools of Rome but succumbed to the practical need for education of its clergy. Although it recognized formal education as a necessary component of preparation for a career as a clergyman, it required that all education be designed with one goal in mind: to enhance faith. With such an objective in mind, it firmly opposed the teaching of science and philosophy.[5]

St. Benedict, founder of the Benedictine Order and a leader in the monastic schools, chose to leave literary study, which he viewed as evil, preferring to be "knowingly ignorant and wisely unlearned." Although he required that monks in his monastery commit to seven hours of manual work and two hours of reading daily, he forbade them to possess pens and books of their own to keep them from the evil temptation of literary study. The crusade against learning even went so far as Pope Gregory's condemnation of grammatical instruction for any person in a monastery.[6]

Despite the negative feelings of the church toward liberal education, there were a few bold teachers who worked to continue the incorporation of secular teaching in monasteries. St. Jerome continued teaching in secular schools even after taking the monastic vows. Cassiodorus, born in 480 in South Italy, developed an interest in the combination of sacred literature and liberal arts. His treatise "Institutiones divinarium et saecularum lectonium" addressed each of the seven liberal arts and became a primary text in monasteries intent on teaching secular knowledge.[7]

One oblate called Gerbert (later known as Pope Sylvester II), the son of a French peasant, brought change and fame to the school of Reims with incredible changes to the previously monotonous monasteries. Although he never sacrificed discipline, Gerbert brought originality and depth to the subjects of the Quadrivium.[8] To arithmetic, he introduced the nine Hindu-Arabic numerals (1, 2, 3, 4, 5, 6, 7, 8, 9), which had previously been confined to Moslem Spain and Sicily in western Europe. Scholars were undoubtedly relieved to escape the myriad mathematical complications associated with multiplication in Roman numerals. He also reintroduced the abacus for use in calculation.[9]

In addition, Gerbert introduced the concept of practical instruction, believing that the theory of any subject should be demonstrated whenever possible in a practical manner. For music lessons, he advocated for the use of instruments. For astronomy, he recommended the use of spheres for viewing the position and movement of the heavenly bodies. He also invented a forerunner of the telescope used for observation of the stars. Gerbert's other major contribution was a renewed emphasis on rhetoric and logic, or public speaking.[10]

Gerbert's fame was so widespread that Otto III—the half-Saxon, half-Greek emperor—requested that Gerbert take a position as his private tutor. Gerbert obliged, and in 997, the two embarked on a mission to revive the spirit of ancient scholarship and restore the glory of Rome.[11] Other royals contributed to a surge in educational opportunities in the West. Charles the Great recognized a need for education to promote progress in his kingdom, and he invited a team of scholars to help bring about reform. He chose to begin with the clergy, noting that it filled an instructional role and would be in the best position to elevate the people.[12]

Charles began by setting churches to the task of correcting the grammar in the copies of Scripture and service books they used. He explained, "Desirous as we are of improving the condition of the churches, we impose on ourselves the task of reviving with the utmost zeal the study of letters, well-nigh extinguished through the neglect of our ancestors. We charge all our subjects, so far as they may be able, to cultivate the liberal arts, and we set them the example."[13]

His success took the form of increased educational opportunity in schools developed in cathedrals and presided over by bishops. The most famous were located at Chartres, Tours, Paris, Rouen, Liege, and Utrect, prompting a description of France as "the oven where the intellectual bread of the whole world was baked."[14] In schools such as these, students studied the seven liberal arts: grammar, dialectic, rhetoric, arithmetic, geometry, astronomy, and music.[15]

These "bishops' schools" came into vogue after the complete disappearance of public schools. Begun by missionaries in England, they followed the logic that to learn the elements of religion, students must first learn Latin grammar, since all services were conducted in Latin. As time progressed and more subjects entered the curriculum of bishops' schools, the bishops themselves began to delegate the teaching responsibility to council members. By the eighth century, these members were both living and teaching in cathedrals.[16] Called *chancellors*, they took on the roles of schoolmasters and taught a curriculum based on the seven liberal arts. Bishops' schools persisted as the main centers of education until the twelfth century.

It is from these schools that the universities of the Renaissance developed, largely because of jealousies and rivalries between masters. One student called Abelard related a tale of jealousy in a letter. Abelard had been well educated in literature from childhood and had traveled Europe, participating in debates and listening to lectures. When he reached Paris and studied under the prominent scholar William of Champeaux, he frequently argued with the master and was therefore met with dislike by leading scholars of the period. Abelard chose to begin teaching his own classes rather than persist as a student, meeting indignation on the part of William, who attempted to separate his pupils from those studying under Abelard.[17]

Situations like this one prompted the formation of universities, from the Latin *universitas*, meaning "guild." Masters banded themselves to protect their rights, producing the well-known schools at Salerno, Bologna, Paril, Montpellier, and Oxford. Also, because of stories such as Abelard's, by 1215, the pope mandated that no lecturer under the age of twenty-one could speak about the arts at Paris, nor could any person who had not studied for at least six years. One had to be at least thirty-five and have studied for eight years to lecture on theology.[18]

So began the institution of university study that we still see today. Many of the characteristics of the universities of the Middle Ages can also still be found today, from the credentials required for professorship to the subjects viewed as essential. Even the progression of study in medieval universities closely resembles the programs offered today. At thirteen or fourteen, a student would enroll and study under a master for three to seven years. After those years of study, he would begin teaching with supervision from the master and continue studying so that he could defend a thesis before the faculty. A successful defense was rewarded with a degree termed the *licentiate, mastership,* or *doctorate,* all synonymous in the Middle Ages. Baccalaureate was regarded as formal admission to be considered for a license and was later defined as a minor degree.[19]

Note that the masters of the universities were not necessarily clergy members. This trend indicates a scholarly lean toward the secular. In the fourteenth and fifteenth centuries, state and church leaders in law, theology, and science were educated by medieval universities.[20] Historian R. Freeman Butts notes, "Secular forces had already become strong in the Middle Ages, but the clue to the Renaissance is that secularism began to permeate Renaissance culture to a greater degree."[21]

As Europe rocketed toward an age of enlightenment, education played a major role and saw significant changes to its structure and content. Scholars and leaders became keenly aware of the restriction of medievalism and began to seek ways to enjoy fuller lives as individuals. Although, in the perspective of history, we tend to view their next step as one of novelty, it seems that they were seeking a return to the glory of the past. Architecture, literature, philosophy, science, and even theology began to mimic the wisdom of ancient Greco-Roman culture. Still, what was born was a world different from both the medieval era and the ancient world.[22]

Francesco Cordasco, author of *A Brief History of Education,* notes that the changes in education during the fourteenth and fifteenth centuries can be traced to two major developments: a revived interest in liberal education and an emphasis on humanism.[23] The former hearkens back to the ancient world and speaks to the desire for a return to that glory. The latter represents a step forward, resulting in an unprecedented freedom for the individual.

In the early Renaissance, the aim of education was revised and became what Cordasco calls "the formation of the man who participated in the activities of the dominant social institutions." In *On Noble Character and Liberal Studies*, written during the early Renaissance by Paulus Vergerius, such an aim was exemplified when the author wrote, "We call those studies liberal that are worthy of a free man; those studies by which we attain and practice virtue and wisdom; the education which calls forth, trains, and develops those highest gifts of body and mind, which ennoble men and are rightly judged to rank next in dignity to virtue only."[24]

Vergerius demonstrates not only a renewed interest in the liberal arts but a new emphasis on what would come to be called *humanism*. Historian John Hale defines humanistic belief noting that "lessons were to shape the pupil's character and prepare him for a life of useful service."[25] According to author Susan Goodenough, humanism also emphasized the value of the individual. She notes that the humanists became enthralled with the translation and study of ancient Greek and Latin books, resulting in a revival of interest in the old ideas.[26]

The dominance of the church over thought and education in the Middle Ages gave way as the increased trade of city centers once again freed scholars to contemplate ancient works and ideas. New theories that the independent mind ought to be celebrated and that life ought to be regarded for its beauty became more commonplace. Still, religion was not completely abandoned. Many believed that a greater appreciation for beauty and life would lead to greater belief in God.[27]

The ideas of the humanists spread rapidly and widely as leaders of the movement taught and encouraged the construction of schools. While English boys began going to the homes of others for education, children in Italy had the opportunity to attend primary and high schools. Students intending to study accounting might take a course in mathematics called the *abacus*. Although much study involved direct memorization, the appearance of slates and hornbooks began to change the face of education, allowing students to practice writing and note taking.[28]

Higher education also experienced changes all too familiar to some of today's teachers. At certain universities, lecturers were threatened with the elimination of any courses attracting fewer than six students, essentially requiring them to make their lectures more interesting. Entrance requirements began to appear in Florence, where students needed a grammar school education to attend.[29]

Further revolution followed the spread of the printed word in the mid-fifteenth century. After the appearance of Gutenberg's Bible in 1456, printing reached Italy and brought about printed editions of a Latin grammar book and selected writings of Cicero, a testament to the value placed on the ancient writings. Soon after, the first book printed in English, a history of Troy, was produced in Bruges, and following that, an edition of Chaucer's *Canterbury Tales* appeared.[30] With increased availability of the written word, it followed naturally that interest in literacy became more widespread. Before long, Bibles, sheet music, and Martin Luther's *95 Theses* were widely available, with the last item selling four thousand copies in only five days.[31]

One can imagine quite easily that the availability of the printed word would revolutionize the act of teaching. While monks had placed such an incredible amount of focus on the meticulous handwritten reproduction of written language, scholars of the Renaissance were able to devote their attention to the study of information that they had not yet seen. Still, there was quite a delay in the spread of literacy even after the advent of the printed word. Since any person, capable or not, could label himself a teacher, there were many instructors below the university level who were able to read but not comprehend or who were unable to decode altogether. For that reason, some city-states instituted the first regulations on schools, requiring that teachers know how to read and write in Latin.[32]

At the grammar school level, teaching techniques remained quite scientific, emphasizing rote memorization. Historian John Hale explains,

> With a few . . . exceptions the emphasis was on learning by rote from antiquated schoolbooks, some of them copied and printed unchanged from the twelfth and thirteenth centuries. Such books—Latin grammars for the most part—were read aloud and copied down sentence by sentence by the pupils, the metrical form into which many of them were cast emphasizing the stress on mere memory training.[33]

A few teachers did deign to experiment in the art of teaching, perhaps pioneering some of the methods explored in later generations. Marineo Siculo, teacher of Spain's noblemen in the court of Queen Isabella, "pushes his students as quickly as possible through the rote-learning of grammatical rules to the texts themselves, to the personalities of their authors; in this way, he claimed 'they will certainly advance more, and become not grammarians but Latinists.'"[34]

Another celebrated teacher of the Renaissance, Vittorino da Feltre, had a remarkable teaching career. Vittorino received a fairly typical medieval education, studying Latin grammar and literature, philosophy, and church law at the University of Padua, financing his education by teaching younger students. He eventually earned his doctorate, then called a *laurea*, and remained at the university where he taught Latin grammar and mathematics until 1422. After a series of moves, Vittorino eventually settled in Mantua, where he educated five children in the court of the marquis.[35]

Vittorino's school—which he called La Giocosa, or "the pleasant house"—provided a setting that Vittorino felt was ideal. It was an enjoyable place to be, and it provided plenty of room for physical activity. Here, he was able to put into practice the ideals of Petrarch and Quintilian, whose essays on education he so admired. Rather than approaching study of the Latin language as a means for learning philosophy and theology, Vittorino opted to begin with basic grammar. His pupils studied Greek and Latin texts one line at a time, stopping frequently to discuss literary style, new vocabulary, and the elements of literature. He sought to help his students become as proficient in Latin as in Italian and to enable them to read enough Greek to understand the classics.[36]

A modern teacher might be reminded of today's whole language school of thought, which emphasizes that reading is best learned through immersion in language through literature rather than through carefully calculated phonics lessons. Although his efforts are reminiscent of the whole language theory, Vittorino's pedagogical style was more consciously engineered to achieve the Renaissance ideal: individuals of personal honesty and civic responsibility—two qualities that Vittorino felt could be learned from study of the classics.[37]

Ultimately, it seems that Vittorino subscribed much more thoroughly to the artistic view of pedagogy. According to professors L. Glenn Smith and Joan K. Smith,

> Vittorino was deeply convinced that education was not simply a matter of intellectual activity. . . . He believed that physical activity was an important part of education, and encouraged students to play games and engage in athletic competition. . . . By involving himself in the extracurricular life of the students, Vittorino hoped to show them that education helped establish moral values as well as communicated knowledge. . . . While he was well-paid by the marquis, he spent almost everything on his students.[38]

Vittorino's passion for the transformation of his students' lives through education and his interest in the education of the whole child seemed to have set him apart from other teachers of his time. Even though Vittorino's methods were anything but typical for the era, they were acknowledged as remarkable and may have served as precursors to the progressive teaching methods centuries later.

Another humanistic educator of particular interest, Desiderius Erasmus, expressed a more liberal view of the educational goal. Erasmus held that the aim of education was social rather than individual, and he insisted that an ideal society must be born of a liberal education. He advocated for early Latin instruction, admitting that children may not find it interesting but appealing to teachers to inspire the young. Besides motivating students, Erasmus held that teachers ought to pay attention to the aptitudes and talents of their students, encouraging them to pursue relevant courses of study. He argued against harsh discipline, instead recommending that unmotivated students be given manual labor tasks. For the young, he suggested the use of games, including one in which students made alphabet cookies to be eaten as they were learned.[39]

Many of Erasmus's ideas would not seem out of place in a modern elementary classroom, but they were quite out of the ordinary for the time. Still, they are symptomatic of a general cultural shift between the medieval and Renaissance eras. The shift in emphasis from the human as a servant of God to the human as an individual lies at the root of Vittorino's and Erasmus's educational theories. Indeed, it was thinkers like these who enabled the forward progression of pedagogy and education in the Western world.

In a world where the humanistic ideals of the Renaissance had been allowed to flourish, many leaders whom we continue to venerate today were masters of the classical education system laid by their European predecessors. In the next chapter, we observe the educational world in what is now the United States, several centuries after the Renaissance.

NOTES

1. Marjorie Rowling, *Everyday Life in Medieval Times* (New York: Dorset Press, 1968), 136.

2. Rowling, *Everyday Life in Medieval Times*, 137.

3. Rowling, *Everyday Life in Medieval Times*, 136.

4. William Boyd and Edmund J. King, *The History of Western Education*, 10th ed. (New York: Harper & Row, 1972), 99.

5. Boyd and King, *The History of Western Education*, 99.

6. Boyd and King, *The History of Western Education*, 99–106.

7. Boyd and King, *The History of Western Education*, 102–3.

8. Rowling, *Everyday Life in Medieval Times*, 139.

9. Rowling, *Everyday Life in Medieval Times*, 140.

10. Rowling, *Everyday Life in Medieval Times*, 141.

11. Rowling, *Everyday Life in Medieval Times*, 142.

12. Boyd and King, *The History of Western Education*, 118.

13. James Bass Mullinger, *The Schools of Charles the Great* (Charleston, SC: BiblioBazaar, 2008), 101.

14. Mullinger, *The Schools of Charles the Great*, 144.

15. Mullinger, *The Schools of Charles the Great*, 144.

16. Boyd and King, *The History of Western Education*, 111–17.

17. H. Rashdall, *The Universities of Europe in the Middle Ages*, vol. 3, ed. F. Powicke and A. Emden (Oxford, UK: Clarendon Press, 1936).

18. Rashdall, *The Universities of Europe*.

19. Francesco Cordasco, *A Brief History of Education* (Totowa, NJ: Littlefield, Adams), 33.

20. Cordasco, *A Brief History of Education*, 34.

21. R. Freeman Butts, *A Cultural History of Western Education*, 2nd ed. (New York, 1955), 165.

22. Boyd and King, *The History of Western Education*, 159.

23. Cordasco, *A Brief History of Education*, 42.

24. Cordasco, *A Brief History of Education*, 43.

25. Patricia D. Netzley, *Life during the Renaissance* (San Diego, CA: Lucent Books), 40.

26. Susan Goodenough, *The Renaissance: The Living Past* (New York: Arco), 30.

27. Goodenough, *The Renaissance*.

28. Goodenough, *The Renaissance*, 31.

29. Goodenough, *The Renaissance*, 31.

30. Goodenough, *The Renaissance*, 23.

31. Goodenough, *The Renaissance*.

32. Netzley, *Life during the Renaissance*, 38–39.

33. Netzley, *Life during the Renaissance*, 40.

34. John Hale, *Renaissance Europe*, 152–53, as seen in Netzley, *Life during the Renaissance*.

35. L. Glenn Smith and Joan K. Smith, *Lives in Education: A Narrative of People and Ideas*, 2nd ed. (New York: St. Martin's Press, 1965), 99.

36. Smith and Smith, *Lives in Education*.

37. Smith and Smith, *Lives in Education*.

38. Smith and Smith, *Lives in Education*, 100.

39. Smith and Smith, *Lives in Education*, 113.

FOUR

Teaching in Colonial America and the Education of the Founding Fathers

The education of children in colonial America varied dramatically throughout the colonies. During the period from the founding of the first colonies until the American Revolution, what and how children were taught depended on a number of factors, including the race and gender of the student as well as the social class of the parents. In addition, religious affiliation could affect the manner of teaching, but perhaps most important was the location of the student's home.

Education in the New England colonies was mainly universal, although the methods used were not always the same. For most children, formal education began at home. Especially for the Puritan church in New England, the goal was to ensure that children were sufficiently literate to read the Bible. There was also the objective of teaching positive "values, manners, social graces, and even vocational skills."[1]

As communities developed in New England, some mothers established schools in their homes. For a fee, a small group of multiaged children were taught reading, writing, and simple math. Called *dame schools*, these were the first organized schools in North America.[2] Following their early experiences at home or as students at a dame school, many boys became apprentices to skilled craftsmen. These boys, as young as seven, lived in the homes of master craftsmen to learn not only the trade but also English and mathematics. As part of their training, they were also taught how to manage a business.

Upon completing their apprenticeships, which might last until they were twenty-one, the young men were then considered *journeymen*. The final stage of the process had the craftsman become a master, who was eligible to take on apprentices. Girls stayed at home, where they learned homemaking skills from their mothers; most were also taught reading as well as some simple math.

As early as 1647, the Massachusetts Bay Colony General Court passed a decree that attempted to require all towns containing more than fifty residents to "appoint a master to teach all children to read and write and that all communities with more than one hundred residents."[3] However, this initiative did not create a universal public education system in Massachusetts.

Even after the American Revolution, the state legislature of Massachusetts found it necessary to pass a law in 1789 that again gave responsibility for establishing schools to the local towns. In most cases, what had emerged in many communities were schools managed by churches or the local community government. The creation of the common school did not remove religion from the schools in the state, as students were still taught using the Bible and were instructed in the specific beliefs of the Puritan church.[4]

When Horace Mann accepted the new position of secretary of education in Massachusetts in 1837, he described the status quo at that point:

> In this Commonwealth, there are 3,000 public schools, in all of which the rudiments of knowledge are taught. These schools, at the present time, are so many distinct independent communities; each being governed by its own habits, traditions, and local customs. There is no common, superintending power over them; there is no bond of brotherhood or family between them. They are strangers and aliens to each other. As the system is now administered, if any improvement in principles or modes of teaching is discovered by talent or accident, in one school, instead of being published to the world, it dies with the discoverer. No means exist for multiplying new truths, or preserving old ones.[5]

In these schools, Mann found the children being lectured to, and when the teacher had completed the lesson, students were lined up to stand in front of the professor and repeat what had been taught. Time was taken each day for the students and the teacher to kneel in prayer and for each child to recite the day's biblical lesson. It was not unusual for students whose recitations were unsatisfactory to be physically punished. Neither parents nor students were surprised if a child went home with "welts and bruises, marks left by a teacher's rod."[6]

In one-room classrooms, there would most often be separate benches for boys and girls. The multiaged students would frequently take turns reading a passage from the Bible. Schooling for girls, prior to the American Revolution at least, might well be concluded after one or two years. Still, it was important to parents that the girls also learn to read the Bible, as it was thought that it would make them better wives and mothers.

The teaching techniques in New England colonial schools were structured, and memorization was important. Along with their teaching responsibilities, teachers were expected to be building custodians and undertake the challenging task of maintaining order in their classrooms. To do this, some schoolhouses even had whipping posts in the classrooms or schoolyards. This was accepted in Puritan communities because their faith taught that "children were born sinful."[7] A less violent "punishment" that was often effective was to force a misbehaving boy to sit with the girls. This practice was known in some schools as *capital punishment.*[8]

While teaching methods did vary from town to town, a common problem was irregular attendance. It was also true that, other than the Bible, there was often no established curriculum. Teachers had no formal training in how or what to teach, and they made up their lessons from what they knew and from the books that they had on hand.[9] By far, the most common books used were the *New England Primer, Noah Webster's Spelling Book,* and *McGuffy's Reader.* A frequent visual aid used in many classrooms was the *Horn Book,* which was "shaped like a mirror and had attached to its frame a sheet of paper containing the alphabet, Lord's Prayer, and numbers."[10]

Schools during the colonial period had no blackboards, although a few might have had globes. There were no slates or lead pencils, and students were forced to use goose-quill pens and ink, provided by their families. Paper was scarce and expensive. Even so, the students appear to have been competent at handwriting. From available samples, they were more capable at this skill than many modern American students. Yet, less attention was paid to correct spelling.[11]

For upper-class boys, there was the opportunity to continue learning at Latin grammar schools. These young men began to attend such schools at age seven or eight and continue as students until fifteen or sixteen, when they were ready to apply for college. The Latin grammar schools were also modest one-room structures. The teachers were men called *masters,* who often had some college education. Teaching in tuition schools for upper-class boys offered more prestige and higher salaries than teaching in the churches or village elementary schools.

Because the entrance tests for Harvard and Yale required competency in Latin and Greek, these subjects dominated the curriculum. Students studied the ancient Roman writers, including Cicero, Caesar, Virgil, and Horace. More advanced students would be introduced to such Greek writers as Socrates and Homer. Some schools also included instruction in a broader curriculum that might include reading and writing about mathematics, astronomy, ethics, some English authors, and even surveying or bookkeeping.[12]

In all the schools in New England, it is important to note that there was a major emphasis on Christian teaching. It is also true that in New

England, there was a shared commitment regarding the responsibility of teaching children. It was generally agreed on that the home, the church, and the school needed to be part of developing good parents and citizens. As most of the New England population had emigrated from England, it came with a strong belief in the value of education. The religious reformation in Europe had "made reading an essential part of religious observances."[13]

There was a shared belief among the English colonists that learning was a means to improve one's life. For historian Lawrence Cremin, families were the most important partners in providing education to children. Along with education at home, families in a community spent a considerable amount of time in a church that saw teaching "the best ways to live" as its goal. For most of the colonial period and for most children, schools had less impact on child development than either the home or the church.[14]

One of the problems faced by all sections of the country during this period of our history was a lack of qualified teachers. Although maybe one in four of Harvard's seventeenth-century graduates did teach for one or two years, most were merely "waiting for a congregation to call them as a minister, but barely three percent of people holding college degrees had lifetime careers in education, usually as masters at the better grammar schools."[15]

Overall, the schools for young children in New England were inefficient and failed to reach all children. Still, it was undoubtedly true that the rate of literacy in this section was higher than either in the middle colonies or in the South.

In the middle colonies, the schools were more varied because a number of Christian churches were available to the citizens. Schools were established by Anglicans, Quakers, Catholics, Mennonites, Huguenots, and members of the Dutch Reformed Church. There was also a more diverse ethnic population in many colonies. Settlers who came from Germany or Sweden frequently wanted to set up their own schools, called *private venture schools*. These schools were licensed by towns and financed by parents. In such schools, parents made contracts with and personally paid the teachers.[16]

Just as in New England, schools in the middle colonies stressed religion, but there were, in some cases, special training in practical subjects, such as navigation and bookkeeping.[17] The church-sponsored schools were often taught by ministers, and even if a nonclergyperson was hired, that person would be carefully supervised by the clergy. Such a teacher might also earn extra compensation as a choir master, a member of the chorus, a bell ringer, or a custodian.[18]

In a move toward a more universal education system, the denomination known as the Society of Friends, or the Quakers, opened its schools not only to both genders but to African American and Native American children.[19] In regard to African Americans, such a practice would have been illegal in the Southern colonies, where educating slaves was a serious crime. The plantation system that developed in the South created a different setting for education. For example, in Virginia, where the upper class was primarily plantation owners, males were given a "traditionally English type of education," which began with tutoring at home.

Individual teachers were brought in and often worked one-on-one with a son of a plantation owner. They were taught not only basic academic skills but "social graces and good manners." Daughters in these families learned at home how to be successful hostesses. For most of the poor white farmers, education was the responsibility of the parents, apprenticeships, or, in some cases, "charity-provided pauper schools." For most of these children, formal education lasted only a few years.[20]

Most historians would agree with the assertion of Ryan and Cooper in their textbook *Those Who Can, Teach*. Their conclusion regarding education in the South was that "the great distances between southern settlements encouraged plantation owners to educate their children with private tutors, who were often local ministers or itinerant scholars. In addition, most southern settlers were members of the Anglican Church and did not share the Puritan belief that everyone had a religious obligation to learn to read."[21] Despite the limited educational opportunities available in this section of our country, a number of the most important figures in our colonial history benefited from a superior education.

In a book written in 1973 entitled *Seven Who Shaped Our Destiny*, Richard B. Morris identified the most important of our founding fathers as being Thomas Jefferson, James Madison, George Washington, Benjamin Franklin, Alexander Hamilton, John Jay, and John Adams.[22] Of this group, three were products of Southern education. Perhaps the best example of the type of education that was possible for the sons of plantation owners was the educational experience of Thomas Jefferson, who in many ways could be considered a "Renaissance man."

John Kennedy spoke about Jefferson at a White House dinner honoring Nobel Prize winners and was quoted as saying, "I think this is the most extraordinary collection of talent, of human knowledge, that has ever been gathered together at the White House—with the possible exception of when Thomas Jefferson dined alone."[23] Richard B. Morris classified Thomas Jefferson as "a true product of the enlightenment" who "cultivated his restless mind in every known branch of knowledge." Besides government, he was well versed in history and classical literature, as well as architecture, science, and music.[24]

His education began at age five with a tutor who worked only with his family. At age nine, his father enrolled him in a Latin school operated by the Reverend William Daulas, an Episcopal or Anglican clergyman. Living in the minister's home, the young man learned the rudiments of Latin, Greek, and French. Jefferson later criticized his tutor as being "but a superficial Latinist" who was "less instructed in Greek." When he reached the age of fourteen, Jefferson transferred to the school of another Anglican clergyman, the Reverend James Maury. Both the character and the learning of this man impressed Jefferson, who described him as "a correct classical scholar."

In a 2012 biography of Jefferson, John Meacham refers to Reverend Maury's defense of the study of the classic languages. The tutor wrote, "It would not be necessary for every young person to study the classics, but that 'an acquaintance with the languages spoken in ancient Greece and Italy is absolutely necessary for those who wish to make any reputable figure in divinity, medicine, or law.'" He went on to argue that classical training was "also critical for men who might take a place in society." Jefferson agreed and continued to read the classics throughout his life. [25] It is interesting to note that modern educators have reached the conclusion that the study of the ancient languages is no longer necessary, and as a result, Latin has disappeared from the curriculum of the majority of high schools in America.

Jefferson continued his education at William & Mary College, where he was greatly influenced by several professors. The first was Dr. William Small, whom Jefferson credited with "influencing the destinies of my life," as he was a teacher who was "profound in most of the branches of science" but who also had a "happy talent of communication and a correct and gentlemanly manner and an enlarged liberal mind." [26]

While at William & Mary, Jefferson was said to have studied fifteen hours a day and to have spent most of the rest of his time exercising. Still, he had time to devote to a social education that occurred in large part in the palace of the English governor, where he benefited from the opportunity to learn proper manners as well as how to engage in intelligent academic and political conversations. The final segment of his formal education came as he studied law with George Wythe, a man who became his mentor and friend. In referring to his trusted teacher, Jefferson quoted Euripides, writing, "There is nothing better than a trusted friend, neither wealth nor princely power . . . when set off against a noble friend." [27]

If Jefferson benefited from rich educational opportunities, so did his lifelong friend James Madison. While many of the sons of plantation owners spent much of their youths "riding, hunting, and drinking," James Madison sat reading in his father's rather limited library. For his first ten years, he was educated at home with his many siblings. There were twelve children, seven of whom lived into adulthood. At age eleven, the somewhat small and sickly Madison was sent to the boarding school of Donald Robinson to be privately tutored. By the time he was eighteen, he was ready to begin his college education at The College of New Jersey, which later became Princeton University.

Instead of the usual three years of undergraduate study, he completed his bachelor's degree in two years and continued his emphasis on learning the classics as well as studying philosophy and science. Early in his academic career, Madison gained a lifelong interest in government and politics. His study of the great European political philosophers, especially John Locke, would be instrumental in his work at the Constitutional Convention and as one of the primary authors of the Federalist Papers.[28]

George Washington was not as fortunate as Jefferson and Madison. One story regarding his first tutor was that the man was a "convict servant whom his father brought over as a schoolteacher." Although there is no conclusive evidence of this assertion, it is true that some educated convicts came to America as indentured servants. A more likely possibility is that the young Washington attended, for a time, a school operated by the Reverend James Marye. In any case, between the ages of seven and eleven, he did learn to read and write, as well as how to be a surveyor. It appears that he did learn some Latin and have the opportunity to read a number of English authors. Unlike that of his fellow Virginian founding fathers, his formal education was minimal. Throughout his adult life, he avoided "abstract debate" but did learn to be a proficient writer.[29]

Like Washington, Benjamin Franklin spent very little time in formal learning situations. Initially, the family planned for him to study for the ministry. To ensure his proper preparation for later enrolling at Harvard, Ben was sent to Boston at age eight to enter the Latin school where the famous Massachusetts preacher Cotton Mather had received his early education.

Despite the fact that young Franklin was at the top of his class, his father changed his mind about the young man's future. In considering the reason for this decision to end his son's formal schooling, it is possible that Josiah Franklin concluded that his son was not meant for the ministry. Walter Isaacson, in his biography of Franklin, described the young man's youthful personality as "skeptical, puckish, curious, irreverent and impish." No one described the young student as being either "pious or faithful." After his time in the Latin school, Ben was sent to a reading and writing school run by a "businesslike" master, George Brownell. Here, Franklin excelled in writing but did poorly in mathematics.[30]

That he did not follow a college entrance–type program may have made it possible for him to retain his "spontaneity, initiative . . . zest, freshness, and the unclutteredness of his mind." When he was ten years old, after only two years of formal education, Franklin was brought home to work full-time in his father's candle shop. The young man quickly made it clear that he disliked the work, and his father began to fear that Ben would "break loose and go to sea."[31]

After considering a number of trades, Franklin was apprenticed to his twenty-one-year-old brother, James, at age twelve. James had just returned from England, where he had learned printing, and the plan was that young Ben would be an indentured apprentice until he was twenty-one.[32] After several years, James launched his weekly newspaper, called *The New England Courant*. This publication gave the young apprentice an outlet for his first published writing. Like all the founding fathers, Franklin was an avid reader, and as a twelve-year-old apprentice, he was reading books such as Bunyan's *Pilgrim's Progress* and Plutarch's *Lives*.

As a result of his reading, he adopted the process used by Socrates of building an argument through gentle queries. "By asking what seemed to be innocent questions, Franklin would draw people into making innocent concessions."[33] Using this style, he became an effective journalist whose work was frequently discussed by the reading public in Boston. After a crisis regarding the paper, which had begun to be considered overly critical of religion, Ben lost his right to publish his own work and was returned to the role of apprentice printer "subject to occasional beating, rather than a brother and fellow writer."[34] As a result, Franklin decided it was time to move on, and he ran away, eventually settling in Philadelphia.

Although he continued through his long life to read, study, and eventually become a world-famous scientist and political leader, he was, like Washington, a person who had little formal education. This was also true for the early years in the life of Alexander Hamilton. Born on the Caribbean island of St. Croix, he had little or no formal schooling as a young boy — possibly because "his illegitimate birth may have barred him from Anglican instruction." He later shared with his son that he had been tutored for a time by a Jewish woman. His Huguenot mother also most likely taught him French, and as a result, he was more comfortable with the language than any of the other founding fathers who spent a number of years in France.[35]

Prior to attending college, Alexander Hamilton was, for the most part, self-taught, but like the other leaders of this generation, he read widely and even wrote poetry. It was a minister who first took notice of the young man's brilliance. Hugh Knox, who had studied at The College of New Jersey (Princeton), became not only a teacher but a substitute father for Hamilton, who was working in St. Croix as a clerk. It was Knox who advised Hamilton to move to America. A number of his past employers and relatives raised money for his passage, and Knox arranged for several of his friends to take Hamilton in when he arrived in New Jersey.[36]

At the age of eighteen, he began his new life in the United States and prepared to apply for college. He was able to enroll in an academy in Elizabethtown, whose headmaster, Francis Barber, was a recent graduate of The College of New Jersey. Many of his students would attend The College of New Jersey; therefore, the curriculum was designed to help students meet the entrance requirements. The entrance examination required that young men be familiar with the orations of Virgil and Cicero, as well as Latin grammar. They also had to have enough knowledge of Greek to allow them to translate it into Latin or English.[37]

When he felt ready to apply to college, Hamilton preferred to attend The College of New Jersey, but he requested that he be allowed to move as quickly as possible through the curriculum. This request was not accepted by the president and the trustees, and as a result, the ambitious young scholar chose to attend King's College in New York City, which later became Columbia University. He entered in either late 1773 or early 1774 and graduated by the summer of 1774. While at college, Hamilton first thought about a medical career, but subjects other than science became his favorite. Like Jefferson and Madison, he was an active student who gloried in Greek and Latin literature, rhetoric, geography, history, philosophy, and mathematics.[38]

In addition, the young college student was active in a literary society, which caused him to write academic papers to share with other members. While at King's, the young scholar became active in the colonial protest against the policies of England. When the war began, he became an officer and aid to George Washington. It was not until after the war that he studied law and became an attorney.[39]

Another founding father from New York also was a lawyer and went on to be the first chief justice of the United States. Unlike Hamilton, John Jay was a member of a prominent colonial family and was afforded outstanding educational opportunities. Descended from French Huguenots, his mother taught him the rudiments of English and Latin grammar as a very young man. This was followed by three years of classical education in a Huguenot school in New Rochelle. After additional private tutoring, Jay entered King's College at age fourteen and was described as a "born scholar." Before studying law, he also earned a master's degree. As one considers Jay's educational background, it does not vary greatly from those of his Southern contemporaries Thomas Jefferson and James Madison.[40]

The last of our prominent founding fathers to be considered is John Adams, who followed George Washington as president. Like the others, he first learned at home, but as a young boy, he was sent to a dame school to continue his education using the *New England Primer*. This was followed by a brief period of attendance at a local school where he was taught by a man whom he called "lackluster." During this period in his life, the young man showed little interest in reading, and he thought primarily of someday becoming a farmer. When he complained about the teacher, his father enrolled him in a school taught by Joseph Marsh. There, he became excited about reading Cicero's *Orations*, and he began to take his studies seriously.[41]

By age fifteen, he was judged ready to attend Harvard. At the time of his entrance, only twenty-seven students were in his class, and the entire college faculty included just seven professors. His most important teacher and mentor was John Winthrop, who was able to create in Adams an even greater interest in literature and science. Upon graduation and having given thought to the ministry, Adams decided instead to become a lawyer.

Prior to studying law, he chose to save the necessary funds by working as a schoolmaster in a one-room school. One of his students remembered him as not really having his heart in teaching. This former student suggested that as a master, "Adams spent most of his day at his desk, absorbed in his thoughts or busy writing." The same person admitted that his master seemed to like the children and enjoyed working with them. Like Jefferson, Hamilton, and John Jay, Adams completed his education by studying the law.

Having briefly considered education in colonial America and some of the outstanding products of this system, we now find it possible to make some brief observations. First, note that there was no universal system of schools or teaching and that the benefits of education were available to only a minority of white male children. While upper-class boys were afforded the greatest opportunities, not all of them obtained a college education. The most effective teaching was often done by individual tutors or in small classes in small schools. There was no set curriculum, and teachers had little or no training on how to teach.

The teaching methods used during this period of American history were quite limited. It was primarily the teacher telling or reading to the students what he or she wished to have them know and forcing them to memorize the material. There were few, if any, visual aids used. The early schools did not have blackboards, and even books were few in number. Yet, the fortunate few who had tutors or attended schools taught by college-educated masters could participate in wide-ranging discussions about a great variety of subjects, including history, philosophy, and science.

Even more important, these teachers often became excellent role models for their students, who would look back on their times together as life-changing experiences. Another characteristic of colonial education was the effect by almost all teachers on what we might today call *character education*. For many, this included tutoring in the Christian virtues outlined in the Bible. For almost all children, this was an essential text in the home and in most schools.

At the same time, especially in New England, most children learned to read and write, and many were exposed to some literature and mathematics. Parents played much larger roles in their children's education, and the church was a significant source of learning. Children were not only taught the rudiments of their faith but were also given moral and ethical training both at home and in church. Whether it was at home or at school, physical punishment was part of the learning process.

In thinking about the preparation of the generation of leaders that helped establish the United States, we might conclude that they were all considered intellectually gifted. Most of them had educations in classic literature, and all of them were lifelong readers and writers. Although there was no organized national plan for education during this period, we were fortunate to have some of the greatest leaders in our history emerge to create a new nation. Serious attempts to develop an organized school system and train teachers would not develop until the middle of the nineteenth century. This process is the focus of our next chapter.

NOTES

1. David Miller Sadker and Karen R. Zittelman, "The Multicultural History of American Education," in *Teachers, Schools, and Societies* (New York: McGraw-Hill, 2012), 137.

2. Sadker and Zittelman, "The Multicultural History of American Education," 137.

3. V. T. Thayer, *Formative Ideas in American Education* (New York: Dodd, Mead, 1974), 4.

4. William Hayes, *Horace Mann's Vision of the Public Schools* (Lanham, MD: Rowman & Littlefield Education, 2006), 2.

5. Lawrence A. Cremin, *American Education, the National Experience: 1783–1876* (Cambridge, MA: Harper & Row, 1980), 155.

6. David Miller Sadker and Karen R. Zittelman, "The Multicultural History of American Education," in *Teachers, Schools, and Societies* (New York: McGraw-Hill, 2012), 137.

7. Leslie S. Kaplan and William A. Owings, "The History of American Public Education," in *American Education* (Stamford, CT: Wadsworth, 2011), 96–97.

8. Kaplan and Owings, "The History of American Public Education."

9. H. G. Good, *A History of American Education*, 2nd ed. (New York: MacMillan, 1962), 37.

10. Good, *A History of American Education*, 317–18.

11. Clifton Johnson, *Old-Time Schools and School-Books* (New York: Dover, 1963), 36–38.

12. Kaplan and Owings, "The History of American Public Education," 99.

13. Joseph Watras, *A History of American Education* (Boston: Pearson, 2008), 27.

14. Watras, *A History of American Education*, 27.

15. Thomas L. Purvis, *Colonial America to 1763* (New York: Facts on File, 1999), 240.

16. Kevin Ryan and James M. Cooper, *Those Who Can, Teach* (Boston: Houghton Mifflin, 1995), 151.

17. Ryan and Cooper, *Those Who Can, Teach*, 151.

18. Kaplan and Owings, "The History of American Public Education," 102.

19. Kaplan and Owings, "The History of American Public Education," 102.

20. Kaplan and Owings, "The History of American Public Education," 103.

21. Ryan and Cooper, *Those Who Can, Teach*, 99.

22. R. B. Bernstein, *The Founding Fathers Reconsidered* (New York: Oxford University Press, 2009), 6.

23. Bruce Bohle, ed., *The Home Book of American Quotations* (New York: Gramercy, 1986), 214.

24. Richard B. Morris, *Seven Who Shaped Our Destiny* (New York: Harper & Row, 1972), 118.

25. John Meacham, *Thomas Jefferson: The Art of Power* (New York: Random House, 2012), 13–14.

26. Meacham, *Thomas Jefferson*, 25–26.

27. Meacham, *Thomas Jefferson*, 21.

28. Andrew Burstein and Nancy Isenberg, *Madison and Jefferson* (New York: Random House, 2010), 12.

29. Marcus Cunliffe, *George Washington: Man and Monument* (New York: New American Library, 1958), 34–35.

30. Walter Isaacson, *Benjamin Franklin: An American Life* (New York: Simon & Schuster, 2003), 18–19.

31. Isaacson, *Benjamin Franklin*.

32. Isaacson, *Benjamin Franklin*, 20.

33. Isaacson, *Benjamin Franklin*.

34. Isaacson, *Benjamin Franklin*.

35. Ron Chernow, *Alexander Hamilton* (New York: Penguin Books, 2004), 17.

36. Chernow, *Alexander Hamilton*, 38.

37. Chernow, *Alexander Hamilton*, 42–43.

38. Chernow, *Alexander Hamilton*, 48–52.

39. Chernow, *Alexander Hamilton*, 53.

40. Morris, *Seven Who Shaped Our Destiny*, 153.

41. Morris, *Seven Who Shaped Our Destiny*, 33–35.

FIVE

Teaching in the First Public Schools

No single individual was responsible for creating the public school system in the United States. Thousands of men and women in every state participated in an ongoing campaign to develop a structure that provided a free education to every child. It took almost a century to develop a consensus in every state and community that it was the responsibility of government rather than parents to ensure that every student had the opportunity to obtain an elementary and high school education. Sometimes history simplifies major societal movements by ascribing credit to certain movement leaders. In the case of public schools, the man who has been chosen to be featured in our history books is Horace Mann.

If one were to survey textbooks in search of the leaders in the public education movement, Mann's name would be found most often. For example, the following paragraph is typical, appearing in the high school textbook *The Making of Modern America*, by Leon H. Canfield and Howard B. Wilder:

> The most important figure in the growth of public education was Horace Mann. As secretary of the Board of Education in Massachusetts, he was tireless in his efforts to spread the gospel of free public schools, to widen the list of subjects taught in school, and to improve the training and professional standing of school teachers. He was also important in founding the first normal school for the training of teachers.[1]

Like his contemporary Abraham Lincoln, Mann had a minimal formal education as a child. However, unlike Lincoln, he worked hard to prepare himself for college, and he graduated from Brown University. After becoming a successful attorney, he was a candidate for the Massachusetts House of Representatives. He went on to be elected to the state senate and became its presiding officer. During his years as a state legislator, he

41

was involved in a number of reform activities but developed a primary interest in the field of education.[2]

When the state legislature established a position entitled *secretary of the board of education* in 1837, the job was offered to Horace Mann. Giving up his seat in the state senate as well as a lucrative law practice, he accepted the new role and spent the next twelve years campaigning for the establishment of what are now called *public schools*. His dream was to create elementary schools financed by state and local governments, making them free for all children. Mann spent his years in this office traveling throughout Massachusetts, campaigning for what were called *common schools*.[3]

There was significant opposition to the idea of schools being supported by taxpayers. Adults without school-age children asked why they should pay for the education of someone else's child. Church officials worried that their church-sponsored schools, which charged tuition, would cease to exist and that the common school would be unable to teach the tenets of their denominations' faiths.[4]

Most religious denominations eventually accepted the idea of the common school. Some Roman Catholics objected to the fact that the new public schools used the King James Bible and Protestant hymns and that textbooks seemed to reflect anti-Irish and anti-Catholic biases. New York City Catholics protested the fact that their taxes would be used to finance what they considered "Protestant public schools." One critic said that Catholics "are unwilling to pay taxes for the purpose of destroying our religion in the minds of our children."[5]

When a number of Jewish and Protestant parents joined a crusade to force government to help finance schools run by churches, the issue escalated. The debate, led by Catholic clergy, spread to the newspapers. An editorial in the *New York Herald* argued, "Once we admit that the Catholics have a right to a portion of the school fund, every other sect will have the same right. . . . We shall be convulsed with endless jarrings and quarrels about the distribution of it, and little left for the public schools."[6]

In 1854 in Pennsylvania, the conflict turned violent, and a Catholic church was burned down, leaving thirteen people dead. When it became obvious that a majority of the voters opposed allotting public funds to religious schools, archbishop John Hughes of New York City started a movement to create Catholic schools. This trend spread throughout the nation. These schools would be provided on a tuition basis as an alternative to public schools.[7]

Despite the opposition of some churches, Mann convinced a majority of the voters in Massachusetts that religion would not be ignored in the public schools. He argued that the Bible could remain an integral part of the curriculum and that the only difference would be that in the new common schools, it would not be possible to teach the specific doctrines of any single denomination.

It is interesting that in 2013, the issue of using public money for religious education is still very much alive. Seventeen states are now offering thirty-three programs that allow parents to use government funds to help pay for the cost of private schooling. These programs include those in religious schools. Although there are many approaches, the most common involves the distribution of vouchers to help pay for tuition at private schools. This approach was made possible as a result of a 2002 Supreme Court decision that school vouchers did not violate the U.S. Constitution's separation of church and state.[8]

There were other criticisms of the common school concept. Some factory owners were concerned that young people would not be available to work in their businesses. Mann countered this argument by pointing out that in the future, workers would need to be literate to do their jobs. Another argument that he used was to suggest that in our democracy, it is essential to have literate citizens.

As a result of Mann's leadership, Massachusetts created a significant number of public elementary schools as well as some secondary schools with the help of the state legislature. To improve teaching in these schools, Mann successfully convinced the legislature to establish several teacher-training institutions called *normal schools*, in which instruction was given on how children learn, the organization of curriculum materials, classroom management, and a variety of teaching techniques. Horace Mann was personally opposed to the method of teaching being used in the schools that he observed. What he saw was students working to memorize the textbooks and then recite them to their teachers.[9]

Concerning his teaching methods, Mann must be considered "ahead of his time." He argued that schools should be teaching science, and he believed that the "teacher must take an active, lively part in lessons instead of peering dully into a textbook and asking routine questions which call for memorized replies." Mann "stressed the value of demonstration, of example, of 'visual aids,' which play so large a role in our schools today," all of which was unlike what was occurring in most schools. While many traditional educators criticized his methods, Mann made clear to his audiences his view that "the object of education was not to cram the student with received opinion, but rather to provide him with the means for forming his own reasoned views."[10]

In his reports to the legislature, he emphasized the need for teachers to have "a repertoire of teaching techniques, not only common methods for common minds, but also peculiar methods for pupils of peculiar dispositions and temperaments."[11] To ensure that teachers were well prepared, Mann convinced the legislature to appoint area superintendents to supervise and certify teachers. In addition, he sought to consolidate one-room school houses into multiroom buildings. After a trip to Europe, he favored organizing schools by grade level.[12]

Horace Mann also had a number of ideas regarding what students should be taught. He believed that schools must provide a moral compass for children and that this was the primary duty of public education. In his words, "the schoolroom and its playing-ground, next to the family table, are the places where the selfish propensies come into the most direct collision with social duties. Here, then a right direction should be given to the growing mind."[13]

One might summarize the contributions of this very important educational pioneer as follows:

- Foremost in his vision was that the common school should be free for all children in every community.
- He believed that the common school should teach a moral code based on Christian principles that all denominations could agree on. In doing so, the Bible would be used as the chief text.
- He advised that common schools teach students to love their country and to know and be able to use the common democratic principles agreed on by all political parties.
- He wanted to ensure that teachers understood that teaching was both an art and a science and that they would use varied techniques to meet individual student needs. It was his personal opinion that women were better suited than men to teach younger children. He also insisted that teachers provide strong role models for children and that their personal conduct be above reproach.
- He continued to strive for a system of certification for teachers, either by a local superintendent or by the state board of education. For Horace Mann, the best education for future teachers would be available at state-sponsored normal schools.
- He believed that corporal punishment should be abolished in schools and be replaced by more positive behavior management techniques.
- Schools should be organized by grades, in which children of the same age should be grouped. One-room schoolhouses, in which all age levels were taught simultaneously, would be replaced by larger buildings housing a number of grade levels.
- In terms of the management of the common schools, Horace Mann sought a prominent role for state government. For him, the state should be primarily responsible for developing a common curriculum in the areas of language arts, mathematics, science, history, music, art, and physical education. Although principals and superintendents would be responsible for the day-to-day management of schools, the state government would be responsible for overseeing all phases of school life.[14]

While in some ways, Mann's philosophy dealt with subjective aspects of teaching, he was concerned about testing accountability. In 1845, he supported his friend Gridley Howe, who "masterminded the use of written tests" in Massachusetts. Howe and the School Committee carefully studied the results of a test given to students throughout the state. It is not surprising that the results of the testing program sound similar to what is occurring in the United States in the twenty-first century.

Among the results were "cheating scandals, poor performance by minority groups, the narrowing of the curriculum, the public shaming of teachers, the appeal of more sophisticated measures of assessment, the superior scores in other nations, all amounting to a constant drumbeat about school failure." Furthermore, poor children did less well on the tests than did those with affluent parents. Also similar to our current situation, "the members of Howe's committee were mesmerized by the charms of numbers, tables, and ranked lists." [15]

Another issue that continues to be a challenge today faced the leaders of the common school movement. Especially in the cities, there was an increased diversity in the students that were attending schools. As public elementary schools grew in number, a melting-pot philosophy emerged. Since most of those in positions of authority over the schools were white Protestants, it was the goal in most schools "to create an English-speaking citizenry" with a "value orientation based on Protestant Christianity." The schools were expected to create a general American ethic. [16] For many in the late-twentieth and early-twenty-first centuries, this goal was much too narrow. As a result, schools have been urged by scholars to adopt what is now called a *multicultural education*. This approach emphasizes that schools should celebrate our differences in race, religion, and ethnic background.

Horace Mann's vision for public schools gradually spread across the United States. When he resigned from his position in Massachusetts in 1850, the percentage of white children attending any school varied greatly. Although almost a third of white children in Vermont were at least exposed to some schooling, in California it was less than 1 percent. Michigan would lead the way with public schooling for white children, while the Southern states were well behind. [17] In just 20 years, the percentage of white children attending school had moved to more than 60 percent. Blacks were frequently educated in separate schools, even in the North. The Amish and Mennonites usually chose to educate their children at home. [18]

Even though elementary education was spreading, the student:teacher ratios would be considered very high today. In 1850, one survey suggested that there was one teacher in the United States for every thirty-four students. Vermont had the best class size ratio with one teacher for twenty-two students, while in New Jersey it was for every forty-two students. [19]

While Horace Mann is acknowledged in American history textbooks as the primary leader of the public school movement, most teachers, as well as other prominent educational leaders, were not quick to accept Mann's ideas concerning teaching. It was not until the beginning of the twentieth century and the introduction of progressive education that real change occurred in most schools.

Still, it is true that some changes were taking place in our schools during the post–Civil War era. American textbooks were frequently replacing European education materials that had been used during the colonial period. Sometimes called the "Schoolmaster of the Republic," author Noah Webster's *American Spelling Book* was used to teach generations of students the "rudiments" of the English language. This book was also a means for "helping to unify the country" by teaching all children a common form of the English language. After the *American Spelling Book* was replaced by the popular McGuffy reader series, the emphasis on teaching Greek and Latin in American schools began to decline. This series alone sold more than 122 million copies in the United States.[20]

Historian Joel Spring suggested that a purpose of the McGuffy readers was to not only teach reading and writing but also to introduce children to a common national morality. For this historian, morality was the idea "that if you should work hard and acquire wealth, then you are blessed by God." He cites lesson 40, "Charlie and Rob," in *McGuffy's Third Eclectic Reader*:

> "Don't you hate splitting wood?" asked Charlie. "No, I rather like it," said Rob. "It's a tough job and it's nice to conquer it." Now which of these boys do you think grew up to be a rich and useful man and which of them joined a party of tramps before he was thirty years old?[21]

The education of the minority of students who had the advantage of attending a secondary school varied, but these schools were also undergoing change. As early as 1751, Benjamin Franklin pioneered what was to become a national movement by establishing an academy in Philadelphia. Franklin's school sought to provide boys and girls alike with a tuition school that offered a more practical curriculum than that of the Latin grammar schools. These academies included classes in history, science, and math, but for many, there were also opportunities for students to learn practical occupational skills.[22]

Along with the changes in the books being used, there were extracurricular activities to increase student interest in the curriculum. At every type of school and at every level, a popular academic competition was the spelling bee. Students of all ages struggled with words such as "'argillaceous' (of the nature of clay), 'tetrastoon' (a four-sided court with porticoes), and 'acephalous' (without a head)."[23] Parents would flock to these competitions to cheer on their children.

For many families in the nineteenth century, education of their children was becoming a major priority. Still, historian George S. Morrison wrote that as late as 1910, only 10 percent of American youths attended a secondary school.[24] Other writers have been more positive in their views on the growth of schools in the United States. In *School: The Story of American Education*, the authors point out, "The U.S. was providing more schooling to more children than any nation on Earth." The amount being spent on schools increased from $69 million in 1870 to $147 million in 1890. It was the conclusion of the authors of this book "that the great experiment of universal education was well underway."[25]

Despite the growth of the number of schools, teaching methods were slow to change. As Horace Mann was writing and speaking about ways to improve teaching methods, other leaders continued to defend more traditional methods. Henry Barnard was the first person to hold the title *United States commissioner of education*. Because education was thought to be a constitutional duty of the state and local governments, the federal government did not play a significant role in education prior to the middle of the twentieth century.

Still, Barnard, in his writing and speeches, advocated "that those with sufficient wealth should support public schools as a means of perpetuating their own interest." For him, "capitalistic principles should be inculcated into the minds of the pupils, along with a kind of patriotism that resulted in the worshipping of the traditions and customs of one's country." In regard to minorities, Barnard argued "that it would be cheaper in dollars and cents to educate the Indian than it would be to fight them." As a true conservative, he would preach "moral obedience to the will of the status quo."[26]

Another of the conservative business-minded educational leaders during the period was William T. Harris. A follower of the German philosopher Georg Wilhelm Friedrich Hegel, from whom he "found justification for the prevailing social order and the adjustment of the individual to the mores of the time," Harris believed in the use of traditional teaching methods, which emphasized students learning primarily from textbooks. At the same time, though, he argued that the public school movement was "a means of bringing the people into harmony with the advancement of knowledge." For William E. Drake, the author of *The American School in Transition*, Harris's "emphasis upon the education of the self and the role of reason in the life of the individual may be said to have bridged the gap between Emerson's transcendentalism and the experimentalism of John Dewey."

It is undoubtedly true that many Americans were becoming open to change.[27] By the 1890s, many people in the United States were beginning to question a number of the basic tenets of American society. Partly because of increased industrialism and economic upheaval, people in every social class were considering the possibility that the national belief in laissez-faire capitalism must be altered. Despite the label of the "gay nineties," the final decade of the nineteenth century was, for many, a time of turmoil. In 1893, the nation saw the worst depression in its history.

With the failure of five hundred banks and fifteen thousand businesses and no unemployment insurance, hundreds of thousands of workers were destitute. Many participated in mass protests, including a major march on Washington. The effort of newly formed unions to strike brought about violent confrontations with federal troops.[28]

The problem was not confined to the cities. In the South and Midwest, Populist parties were formed to protest the "dominance of Eastern industrialists, financeers, and railroad tycoons." Many Americans, including a large number who would be considered "middle class," were beginning to question the doctrines of Adam Smith, whose ideas had permeated American thinking since the publication of the book *The Wealth of Nations* in 1776. People were rethinking the need for some government regulations of the economy, and others were questioning the notion of social Darwinism. Earlier in the century, sociologists including Herbert Spencer and William Graham Sumner had taken Darwin's view of evolution, which relied on the survival of the fittest, and used it to explain how society operated. Because they believed that their theory of social Darwinism was a scientific law, they opposed any government activities that interfered with what they saw as the natural order of society.[29]

As Americans faced the new century, these and other pillars of the American belief system were coming under fire. What followed in the first two decades of the twentieth century were later referred to in the history books as the *progressive era*. Among those institutions to be questioned were the schools and the ways that children were taught. This period is the subject of our next chapter.

NOTES

1. Leon H. Canfield and Howard B. Wilder, *The Making of Modern America* (Boston: Houghton Mifflin, 1952), 259.

2. William Hayes, *Horace Mann's Vision of the Public Schools* (Lanham, MD: Rowman & Littlefield Education, 2006), 9–10.

3. Jonathan Messerli, *Horace Mann: A Biography* (New York: Knopf, 1972), 12–15.

4. Messerli, *Horace Mann*, 246.

5. Sheila Curran Bernard and Sarah Mondale, *School: The Story of American Public Education* (Boston: Beacon Press, 2001), 34.

6. Bernard and Mondale, *School*, 36.

7. Bernard and Mondale, *School*, 35–36.

8. Fernanda Santos and Motoko Rich, "With Vouchers, States Shift Aid for Schools to Families," *New York Times*, March 27, 2013, http://www.nytimes.com/2013/03/28/education/states-shifting-aid-for-schools-to-the-family.html.

9. "Horace Mann," http://people.uncw.edu/smithrw/200/Mann.htm.

10. Fred Reinfled, *The Great Dissenters* (New York: Bantam Books, 1960), 55.

11. Robert Badolato, "The Educational Theory of Horace Mann," http://www.newfoundations.com/GALLERY/Mann.html.

12. "Module 5: Common School Reform, 1830–1850," http://asterix.ednet.lsu/~maxcy/4001_5.htm.

13. Lawrence A. Cremin, ed., *The Republic and the School: Horace Mann on the Education of Free Men* (New York: Teachers College, 1957), 51.

14. Hayes, *Horace Mann's Vision*, 27.

15. William J. Reese, "The First Race to the Top," *New York Times*, April 20, 2013, http://www.nytimes.com/2013/04/21/opinion/sunday/the-first-testing-race-to-the-top.html.

16. L. Dean Webb, Arlene Metha, and K. Forbis Jordan, *Foundations of American Education* (Upper Saddle River, NJ: Merrill, 2000), 177.

17. Rush Walter, *Popular Education and Democratic Thought in America* (New York: Columbia University Press, 1962), 120.

18. Lawrence A. Cremin, *American Education: The National Experience, 1783–1876* (Cambridge, UK: Harper & Row, 1980), 178–80.

19. Cremin, *American Education*, 80–82.

20. George S. Morrison, *Teaching in America*, 4th ed. (Boston: Pearson Education, 2006), 325.

21. Morrison, *Teaching in America*, 325.

22. James A. Johnson, Diann L. Musial, Gene E. Hall, et al., *Foundations of American Education*, 13th ed. (Boston: Pearson Education, 2005), 254–55.

23. Bernard and Mondale, *School*, 58.

24. Morrison, *Teaching in America*, 324.

25. Bernard and Mondale, *School*, 58.

26. William E. Drake, *The American School in Transition* (Anglewood Cliffs, NJ: Prentice Hall, 1955), 221.

27. Drake, *The American School*, 222.

28. John Whiteclay Chambers II, *The Tyranny of Change* (New Brunswick, NJ: Rutgers University Press, 2006), 3–4.

29. Chambers, *The Tyranny of Change*, 5.

SIX

The Progressive Education Movement

As our nation entered the twentieth century, the unrest of the 1890s would help to instigate a period of political reform labeled by American historians as the progressive era. It was a movement that stimulated reform at all levels of government and the economy, as well as in our social institutions, such as schools. Although it is seen as having occurred primarily as a result of middle-class dissatisfaction with the status quo, there was unquestionably leadership at the national level. In his first message to Congress, in December 1901, Republican president Theodore Roosevelt began his speech with these words:

> The tremendous and highly complex industrial development which went on with ever-accelerated rapidity during the latter half of the nineteenth century brings us face to face, at the beginning of the twentieth, with very serious social problems. The old laws and old customs which had almost the binding force of law, were once quite sufficient. . . . They are no longer sufficient. [1]

Democratic President Woodrow Wilson echoed the message in 1913, suggesting, "We have come upon a very different age from any that preceded us. We have come upon an age when we do not do business in the way in which we used to do business." [2] Change was occurring not only at the federal level but also in our schools. In the view of John Whiteclay Chambers II, "the transformation of education in the Progressive Era put schools in the forefront of change. . . . Progressive education revolutionized teaching." Its leading advocate was Columbia University philosopher John Dewey, who stressed the importance of a child's own experience and the need to "learn by doing rather than by rote memorization." [3]

Among the changes that he suggested were "broader and more flexible curricula, less formality in the classroom . . . and the addition of

51

gymnasiums, laboratories, manual arts shops, and rooms for art and music." His goal was to create a more "relevant education that would awaken children to human values and capabilities and instill good moral habits that would serve both them and a changing society."[4]

John Dewey, though often given credit as the leader of the progressive education movement, was not the first to use the term. The phrase was first used at the end of the nineteenth century by those calling for a new approach to teaching. Still, history has given much of the credit to Dewey. This is demonstrated in the following quotation, from the high school American history textbook *The Making of Modern America*:

> A man whose philosophy of education greatly influenced the schools of our times was John Dewey, a professor of philosophy at Columbia University. Until the time of Dewey, the schools of this country had aimed at giving the pupils little except factual knowledge. Dewey argued that a school should be a place where the student learns about life by actually living it. Thus a school had to offer more than book learning. It must give the student contact with nature and community life. It must attempt to develop the child's personality.[5]

John Dewey's background prior to assuming his position as a philosophy professor at Columbia University was instructive. He graduated from high school at the age of fifteen and enrolled in the University of Vermont. After receiving his bachelor's degree, he taught school for two years in Oil City, Pennsylvania. Leaving that position, he briefly took another teaching job in his home state but quickly decided that he would become a graduate student at Johns Hopkins University.[6] Upon completing his doctoral work, he taught at several colleges before taking a position at the newly established University of Chicago. By this time he had written several books, but it was here that he would have the opportunity to test the ideas he was writing about.

Dewey was instrumental in creating a laboratory school that, at the height of its enrollment, had 140 students and 23 teachers. The philosophy governing teaching in the school was that teachers should act more as guides or facilitators of learning rather than merely deliverers of information to their students. Students were regularly engaged in projects related to their current experiences and interests. Four- and five-year-old children were encouraged to structure a model of a home lived in by primitive man, which led to "reading literature, to writing stories, and to drawing pictures as the children sought to discover information and to express what they learned about houses."[7]

For older students, clubs were formed to undertake specialized projects that grew out of needs that the students felt. When it appeared that there was a lack of space for the photography club and debating society to hold their meetings, they decided to build a new clubhouse. In doing so, they experienced all phases of the building process, including "architecture, construction, sanitation, interior decoration, and finance." Using the help of outside experts, they learned to cooperate with other people and to allow "different children to contribute according to their talents and abilities."[8]

Throughout the lab school curriculum, there were real-world experiences in cooking, carpentry, and sewing. Using activities such as these, students were also exposed to math and reading skills. It was also part of Dewey's belief system that punishments should not be used to motivate students. He believed if given activities that they cared about, they would be motivated and become problem solvers rather than individuals who merely memorized the material for the next test. Also important to Dewey was utilizing the scientific method in problem solving.

For Dewey, the scientific process included the following steps:

1. Defining the problem that is raised by some upset, difficulty, or disturbance
2. Observing the conditions surrounding the problem
3. Formulating hypotheses that might solve the problem
4. Elaborating the possible consequences of acting upon several alternative hypotheses
5. Active testing to see which alternative idea best solves the problem[9]

Historian Joel Spring attempts to illustrate the kind of lesson that Dewey believed should be used in our schools. A student or students might express an interest in milk. The teacher would guide the students to the sources of the production, chemistry, and distribution of milk. Groups of students might visit the local dairy and develop a group project on milk for the classroom. During this group study of milk, students might learn chemistry, economics, arithmetic, social history, and cooperation.[10]

After a dispute with college authorities, Dewey left the University of Chicago and spent the rest of his career at Columbia, where he would continue to write and give lectures all over the world. In his books, he often discussed his views on teaching. In *American Education: Building a Common Foundation*, Leslie S. Kaplan and William A. Owings summarize what they saw as Dewey's views about effective teaching. Three factors were paramount in Dewey's thinking: "First, teachers need to understand the learners' interests, problems, and developmental levels. Second, teachers must present knowledge in ways that are relevant and make sense to learners. Third, classrooms should reflect society's highest democratic values: tolerance, cooperation, critical mindedness, and political awareness."[11]

As a young professor writing in *The School Journal*, Dewey stated his criticisms of schools as they were currently operated:

I believe that much of the present education fails because it neglects this fundamental principle of the school as a form of community. . . . The teacher is not in school to impose certain ideas or to form certain habits in the child, but is there as a member of the community to select the influences which shall affect the child and to assist him in properly responding to these influences. . . . Examinations are of use only so far as they test the child's fitness for social life and reveal the place in which he can be of most service and where he can receive the most help.[12]

As Dewey grew older, he never stopped finding fault with how schools were teaching. This is how he viewed the usual methods used in schools:

The traditional scheme is, in essence, one of imposition from above and from outside. It imposes adult standards, subject matter, and methods upon those who are only growing slowly toward maturity. The gap is so great that the required subject matter, the methods of learning and of behaving are foreign to the existing capacities of the young. They are beyond the reach of the experience the young learners already possess. Consequently, they must be imposed. . . . Learning here means acquisition of what already is incorporated in books and in the heads of the elders. Moreover, that which is taught is thought of as essentially static. It is taught as a finished product, with little regard either to the ways in which it was originally built up or to the changes that will surely occur in the future. It is to a large extent the cultural product of societies that assume the future would be much like the past, and yet it is used as education food in the society where change is the rule, not the exception.[13]

John Dewey would undoubtedly have been sympathetic to the attempt to define progressive education contained in the 1918 publication of the Progressive Education Association. Included were the following principles:

I. *Freedom to develop naturally*
      The conduct of the people should be governed by himself according to the social needs of his community, rather than by arbitrary laws. Full opportunity for initiative and self-expression should be provided. . . .

II. *Interest, the motive of all work*
      Interest should be satisfied and developed through: (1) direct and indirect contact with the world and its activities, and the use of the experiences thus gained; (2) application of knowledge gained, and correlation between different subjects; (3) the consciousness of achievement.

III. *The teacher a guide, not a taskmaster*
      . . . Progressive teachers will encourage the use of all the senses, training the pupils in both observation and judgment, and, instead of

hearing recitations only, will spend most of the time teaching how to use various sources of information, including life activities as well as books, how to reason about the information thus acquired, and how to express forcefully and logically the conclusions reached.

IV. *Scientific study of pupil development*

School records should not be confined to the marks given by the teachers to show the advancement of the pupils in the study of subject, but should also include both objective and subjective reports on those physical, mental, moral, and social characteristics which affect both school and adult life and which can be influenced by the school and the home. Such records should be used as a guide for the treatment of each pupil. . . .

V. *The Progressive School, a leader in educational movements*

The Progressive School . . . should be a laboratory where new ideas, if worthy, meet encouragement; where tradition alone does not rule, but the best of the past is leavened with the discoveries of today, and the result is freely added to the sum of educational knowledge.[14]

Since the inception of progressive education, traditional educators have criticized the teaching methods advocated by Dewey and other progressives. According to traditionalists, teachers have a duty to present a well-organized curriculum based on society's agreed-on knowledge: to be meaningful, history must be presented with a chronological method that emphasizes the consensus of historians; instructors in math and science must ensure that students develop the knowledge and skills necessary to understand and utilize these disciplines. For the critics, progressive education methods leave gaps in student knowledge, and as a result, students are not well prepared to pursue additional study.

While Dewey was the center of the debate over progressive education, others were very much involved. Francis Parker actually began supporting change in teaching methods before Dewey. Like Horace Mann, Parker had little formal schooling, and after retiring as a lieutenant colonel at the end of the Civil War, he accepted a teaching position in New Hampshire. This experience created for him a new interest in education, and he traveled to Germany to study at the University of Berlin. When he returned to the United States, he wrote a best-selling book entitled *Talks on Pedagogics*. In considering the class structure that had evolved in the United States, Parker became convinced that children of the affluent were receiving a different education than were those children from less-well-off families.

Because he thought that this was wrong, he argued for a uniform curriculum for all students to provide an equal opportunity for all children to pursue the future of their choice. Among his beliefs was his strong opposition to rote learning and punishment as a means of motivation. He even questioned the practice of giving grades. Like Dewey, he favored experiential-based activities, such as field trips and nature activities. Parker went so far as to eliminate spellers, readers, and grammar textbooks and had students learn word sentences rather than the alphabet or phonetics. As a teacher and administrator, he also experimented with a multidiscipline curriculum that combined subjects such as history and literature. His thinking was perhaps instrumental in creating the subject that we now know as *social studies*, which combines history with geography, political science, economics, and sociology.[15]

Along with Parker, Swiss psychologist Jean Piaget also contributed to the progressive movement.

> Piaget believed that the two fundamental characteristics of children's learning and cognitive development are organization and adaptation. Organization is described as the systematizing of information into meaningful patterns. These patterns are used to structure new information so that it does not seem random or chaotic to the learner. Adaptation is the process of coping, or integrating new information into existing perceptions and patterns. Intelligence for Piaget must follow from our ability to organize and adapt. Like Dewey, Piaget saw human beings as born active, curious, interested in communication, and with a need to assimilate information.[16]

In his writing, he emphasized his belief that children learn differently than adults do. Like other progressive educators, he contended that children retain little when they are forced to learn by a teacher and that they remember most when they are actively involved. In recent years, educators have used the theory to develop what is now called *inquiry-based instruction*. Other historians of the progressive movement associate Piaget's theories with the current educational theory labeled *constructivism*. The premise is that "students would be motivated to learn only if they were active learners, constructing their own knowledge through their own discoveries."[17]

An individual who has been given credit for spreading the theories of Piaget and Dewey was William Heard Kilpatrick, a student of Dewey who served for many years as a professor at Columbia. As a teacher and public speaker, Kilpatrick, unlike Dewey, effectively communicated progressive education ideas to students and the general public. People flocked to his lectures, both at the college and in the community. As an entry in the professor's diary illustrates, he understood his role as a teacher of progressive theory. Perhaps his most lasting contribution to teaching was his introduction of the project method, described as follows:

> Walk into our classroom during project time, and you might see children sprawled on the rug taking notes from books on the habitats of beavers or on medieval life, or two students across the room watching a videotape on Jane Goodall, or others conducting toasts on the aerody-

namics of paper airplanes. Go to the library down the hall (past students rehearsing a play they have written), and you might find members of the other half of the class conducting research on virtual reality or the history of Halloween. If you then go to the computer lab, you'll see, for example, one student inputting survey data while another learns to write a new computer language. In short, you never know what you might experience next, or, most important, what the students might experience next. . . . Discipline problems are minimal because students are interested in what they are doing—they see their pursuits as having *purpose*.[18]

Along with Dewey, the name most frequently mentioned in regard to progressive education is Maria Montessori. A contemporary of Dewey, she was an Italian physician who, early in her career, became interested in teaching children who would today be labeled *special education students*. After successfully experimenting with these difficult-to-teach children, she developed a system that was successful. For the rest of her life, she wrote and spoke about her methods to audiences all over the world.

It was her belief that "all children, particularly from three to six years old, adapt to their environment through guided as well as spontaneous activity. Contrary to traditional approaches whereby the teacher is viewed as the power behind learning, Montessori believed that all children are endowed with an absorbent mind that can integrate all that constitutes their culture. The real power lies in the child's mind." Her teaching method attempts to train a student's "senses through manipulation of three-dimensional objects as well as letters of the alphabet."[19]

As a writer who has studied Montessori, Dorothy Canfield Fisher concluded that the "central idea" behind the Montessori system is "a full recognition of the fact that no human being can be educated by anyone else. He must do it himself or it is never done. And this is true at the age of three and at the age of thirty."[20] Teachers in Montessori schools are trained to emphasize specific objectives, which include

- "to awaken the spirit and the imagination";
- "to encourage the child's normal desire for independence and self esteem";
- "to help him develop the kindness, courtesy, and self-discipline that will allow him to become a contributing member of society"; and
- "to help the child learn how to observe, question, and explore ideas independently."[21]

In Montessori classrooms, one would often see

- sandpaper letters designed to be touched as part of a lesson in learning the alphabet;

- the use of cylindrical blocks to help build "fine motor, analytical, and comparative language skills";
- interactive maps to help learn geography;
- real-world experiences, such as cooking and washing dishes;
- an emphasis on good manners and respect of others; and
- students moving through their activities at their own pace. [22]

The effectiveness of the Montessori movement has sometimes been judged by the individuals who have been a product of these schools. Among those often mentioned are Larry Page and Sergey Brin, the founders of Google; Prince William and Prince Harry of England; Katherine Graham, former owner/editor of the *Washington Post*; Jacqueline Bouvier Kennedy Onassis; and chef Julia Child. [23]

Despite the success of many of the students of the Montessori schools, there was not always agreement on the best methods to be used for progressive teaching. John Dewey was sometimes critical of the Montessori method as being too prescriptive and inflexible, yet there is little question that both methods were in agreement "that schools should place a high priority on fostering the curiosity and creativity of children. Both would be critical of 'mindless memorization' and would instead seek to develop students to 'become self-confident, independent thinkers who learn because they are interested in the world and are enthusiastic about life.'" [24]

Even though progressive ideas did influence how students were taught at the beginning of the twentieth century, traditional methods were still the major approach to teaching in most schools. A simplified way of understanding the differences between traditional and progressive teaching is shown in the table.

Although this chart seems to provide some clear-cut differences between the two approaches to teaching, there are extremes in both the traditional camp and the progressive camp. Dewey himself criticized experiments that developed totally unstructured classrooms that "sought to liberate the child from adult authority and social controls." He labeled some of these efforts "progressive extremists" because he believed that these "laissez-faire" approaches had a negative effect on schools. [25]

At least one historian has concluded that the progressive education trend was primarily a product of "an intellectual movement, popular among professors and their doctoral students, especially at Teacher's College at Columbia University, and later at Ohio State University and the University of Illinois." For this scholar, the impact on schools and teaching was minimal, except in a growing number of progressive schools, many of them private. [26]

Others pointed to the fact that even in the public schools, progressive ideas did influence how children were taught. This might be particularly true in the field of early childhood and elementary education, where

Table 6.1.

Traditional Philosophy	Contemporary Progressivism
The specific curriculum and educational outcomes, as well as the majority of the classes to be taken, are prescribed by the state or local district.	The curriculum is more flexible and is influenced by student interest.
Teachers have as their primary function introducing students to content knowledge and skills as outlined in the mandated curriculum.	Teachers are facilitators of learning who provide a learning environment in which students can use a wide variation of activities to learn, in large part, through discovery.
The tools used by teachers are primarily textbooks and workbooks. Today these are often being supplemented by the use of technology, such as PowerPoint presentations.	Progressive teachers use a wider variety of materials and activities that allow individual and group research. This often includes the utilization of community resources.

Source: "The Ongoing 'Education Wars,'" http://www.ceopa.org/Education-Wars.html.

"learning by doing" theories became somewhat popular. At the secondary level, public schools increasingly included science laboratories and other nontextbook learning methods. Furthermore, progressive education began to become more influential within teacher-training institutions.

These normal schools increasingly included in their curricula a variety of teaching methods that might be used to engage children. Attempts were made to help teachers diagnose the needs and interests of children and to connect students in a personal way to their learning. Even so, historian Lawrence Cremin argues that the movement was unable to provide a uniform theory, which eventually reduced its effectiveness.[27]

The battle to determine how our children should be taught was a prominent issue in the nineteenth century as states and individual communities established teacher-training institutions. The effect of these schools on teachers is the topic of our next chapter.

NOTES

1. Louis Paul Todd and Merl Curti, *1865–Present*, vol. 2 of *The Rise of the American Nation*, 3rd ed. (New York: Harcourt-Brace Jovanovich, 1972), 310.

2. Todd and Curti, *1865–Present*, 315.

3. John Whiteclay Chambers II, *The Tyranny of Change* (New Brunswick, NJ: Rutgers University Press, 2006), 102.

4. Chambers, *The Tyranny of Change*, 102.

5. Leon H. Canfield and Howard B. Wilder, *The Making of Modern America* (Boston: Houghton Mifflin, 1962), 599.

6. L. Glenn Smith and Joan K. Smith, *Lives in Education* (New York: St. Martin's Press, 1994), 287.

7. Joseph Watras, *A History of American Education* (Boston: Pearson, 2008), 201.

8. Watras, *A History of American Education*, 201.

9. R. Freeman Butts and Lawrence A. Cremin, *A History of Education in American Culture* (New York: Holt, 1953), 346.

10. Joel Spring, *American Education* (Boston: McGraw-Hill, 1998), 245.

11. Leslie S. Kaplan and William A. Owings, "The History of American Public Education," in *American Education* (Stamford, CT: Wadsworth, 2011), 130.

12. John Dewey, "My Pedagogic Creed," http://www.infed.org/archives/e-texts/e-dew-pc.htm.

13. Newton Edwards and Herman G. Richey, *The School in the American Social Order* (Boston: Houghton Mifflin Company, 1963), 543–44.

14. Margaret Patricia Meyer, *The Development of Education in the Twentieth Century* (New York: Prentice Hall, 1949), 71–72.

15. L. Glenn Smith and Joan K. Smith, *Lives in Education* (New York: St. Martin's Press, 1994), 280–81.

16. John D. Pulliam and James J. Van Patten, *History of Education in America* (Upper Saddle River, NJ: Merrill, 1991), 172–73.

17. Diane Ravitch, *Left Back: A Century of Battles over School Reform* (New York: Touchstone, 2000), 441.

18. Alfie Kohn, *The Schools Our Children Deserve* (Boston: Houghton Mifflin, 1999), 137.

19. Roselle K. Chartock, *Educational Foundations: An Anthology* (Upper Saddle River, NJ: Prentice Hall, 2000), 87.

20. Chartock, *Educational Foundations*, 87.

21. Sierra Montessori Academy, "Montessori Educational Philosophy," http://www.sierramontessori.org/EducationalPhilosophy.htm.

22. Paige Hobey, "The Montessori Story," http://www.chicagoparent.com/magazines/archives/2005/the-montessori-story.

23. "Montessori Graduates," http://mariamontessori.com/mm/?page_id=571.

24. Sierra Montessori Academy, "Montessori Educational Philosophy."

25. Alan C. Ornstein, *Teaching and Schooling in America* (Boston: Pearson Education, 2003), 317–18.

26. Ornstein, *Teaching and Schooling in America*, 317–18.

27. Ornstein, *Teaching and Schooling in America*, 319.

SEVEN

The Normal School and the Evolution of Teacher Education in the United States

Although several private schools in the United States sought to prepare teachers at the end of the eighteenth century, the first publicly supported teacher-training institutions, called *normal schools*, were opened in Massachusetts in 1839. The founder of these schools, Horace Mann, had a vision to create "a new kind of school, a new kind of profession, the principle of taxpayer support, and a new vocation for women: these innovations were represented at the Lexington Normal School, opened on a rainy July day in 1839."[1]

As the idea spread, many regional variations of the curriculum were used in normal schools. In Massachusetts and the other New England states, the European model was followed fairly closely. Students were introduced to the following topics:

- A review of the branches of knowledge
- An introduction to the art of teaching
- Background in the policies governing schools
- A study of a model school[2]

The training was focused on preparing teachers for the newly emerging common schools, or what we today call *elementary schools*.[3] A careful examination of these early teacher-training schools led to the conclusion that specific training in teaching methods was limited. Character training was perhaps the primary goal in these schools. In Massachusetts, the state legislature made clear to teachers that it was their duty "to impress upon their students the principles of piety, justice, and a sacred regard to truth, love of their country, humanity, and universal benevolence, sobriety, industry and frugality, chastity, moderation and temperance, and those other virtues which are the ornament of human society, and the basis upon which a republican constitution is founded."[4]

In addition, the Bible was prescribed "as a daily text for normal school students," as it provided "the rule of life and the means of salvation." Although the state board of education emphasized that normal schools were not sectarian, it was taken for "granted that Protestant Christianity was the common creed of Massachusetts citizens."[5]

While the enrollment of teacher-training schools would grow to seventy thousand students by the beginning of the twentieth century, in 1861, at the outbreak of the Civil War, there were only eleven normal schools in the United States. There were none in the South until the 1870s, when they were created with separate schools for teachers in black schools and white schools.[6]

The buildings used to house these new teacher-training schools were built with as little capital as possible, and most were poorly equipped. Entrance requirements for students varied but were not demanding in any state; they could vary from a minimum of a fourth-grade education to a high school diploma. There was a minimum age requirement of sixteen, however, and all students had to be certified for good moral character. An entrance examination was frequently required on the common branches of knowledge taught in the common schools. Many applicants entered the normal school with prior teaching experience.[7]

In many ways, the curriculum in normal schools was similar to that being taught in academies or what would later become public high schools. The only difference was the portion of the curriculum dealing with pedagogy. Because normal schools developed outside the structure of the established universities, graduation from one of these schools failed to carry the same prestige as a university diploma. Even a hundred years after the formation of the first normal school, only 18 percent of the graduates of teacher-training institutions had four years of college education.[8] It was not until the beginning of the twentieth century that a high school diploma was required to enroll in a normal school. By then, every teacher-training institution had begun to require student teaching, often in a laboratory elementary school affiliated with the normal school.[9]

The early normal schools were frequently located in rural areas, and they attracted students who might not otherwise have sought further education. For more affluent families, children were most often sent to colleges or universities providing a classical education. Most of these families did not consider teaching as a prestigious occupation, especially for their sons. Also, the poor salaries of teachers were not attractive to students growing up in wealthy families.[10]

Even though students often entered normal schools with inadequate academic preparation, they were still introduced to new theories concerning teaching. In 1847, David Perkins Page, a colleague of Horace

Mann, wrote an influential book entitled *Theory and Practice of Teaching*, which would become a classic text in normal schools. For fifty years, this book would be "the essential basis for courses in general education in most normal schools in the United States."[11]

How much of this book or any other book on teaching that a student might be exposed to depended greatly on the length of one's enrollment in the normal school. During much of the nineteenth century, the time spent in training future teachers ranged from one to four years. The requirements for earning state certification increased each decade.[12]

It would be inaccurate to conclude that there was a consensus on how children should be taught during the nineteenth century in the United States. The same kinds of conflicts that we are currently debating in the twenty-first century were present among educators 150 years ago. As early as the 1860s, Johann Heinrich Pestalozzi introduced what we now consider the progressive teaching methods, and they would emerge in the early-twentieth century in the work of Maria Montessori.[13]

Pestalozzi believed that teaching should begin "by presenting simple forms, and the primitive and more distinct colors. Once familiar with these, the children are led to trace the objects of nature about them, and lastly to observe their various resultant combinations. . . . From concrete, they are led to the abstract . . . and are now prepared to form clear conceptions of things they have never seen, through the medium of things they have seen."[14]

By 1861, the normal school in Oswego, New York, was teaching Pestalozzi's theories.[15] Despite the ongoing influence of progressives such as Pestalozzi, the curriculum in most normal schools remained traditional. The classes taught in the normal schools of the state of Connecticut offer a typical breakdown. Twenty percent of the students' time was spent on what were called *professional subjects*. These included such classes as the principles of education, professional ethics, psychology, introduction to teaching, and school management. Fifty-five percent of their program was devoted to what were called *subject matter courses*. Those listed were oral and written English, reading and literature, history, geography, arithmetic, science, music, and art. Finally, 20 percent of the curriculum was spent actually working with students.[16]

It is quite interesting that this breakdown, developed in 1923, is not significantly different from what is used to prepare teachers in many colleges today. Also contained in early documents outlining the goals of normal schools is a reference to what one author labeled "the science of education and the art of teaching."[17] The argument concerning the nature of teaching grew quite heated at the end of the nineteenth century. As the discipline known as *psychology* was added to college curriculums, some thought that educational psychology could furnish teachers with information that would become the basis of a new science called *education*.

G. Stanley Hall believed that the "systematic studies of children" could provide a new and improved basis for educational practice. Such an approach could "place education for the first time on a scientific basis, and be the center around which the education of the future will be organized." [18] Those who thought that this was a possibility sought to develop "a science of education" by systemizing the rules of teaching. [19] William H. Payne "argued that psychology 'stands in the same relation to teaching as anatomy does to medicine.'"

Some were outspoken critics of the idea of education as a science. Two Harvard professors, William James and Josiah Royce, led the debate. James made the argument that "you make a great, a very great mistake, if you think that psychology, being the science of the mind's laws, is something from which you can deduce definite programs and schemes and methods of instruction for immediate schoolroom use." Royce made the argument in a different way when he wrote, "You will degrade science — not help your children — if you persist in seeing only the 'scientific aspects' of your pedagogy. True pedagogy is an art. . . . There is no universally valid science of pedagogy that is capable of any complete formulation and of application to the individual pupils and teachers. . . . In short, 'there is indeed no science of education.'" [20]

Another approach to the argument about the nature of teaching is contained in the work of Joseph Axelrod. For him, there are two types of teaching. The *didactic* mode emphasizes the teacher's role in the passing on of "traditional knowledge or lore, or teaching how to do something." He describes the didactic form of teaching as follows:

> Teachers use lecture to inculcate knowledge or demonstration to model actions, after which students demonstrate that they have learned, which was taught either by reciting or writing the material or by repeating the demonstration, as in a science class experiment. Much state and national testing relies on rote recall of material. In this context, learning means being able to reproduce what has been taught or demonstrated. For example, students should recall key facts of American history such as the order of the American presidents. [21]

Certainly, most teaching in early America would have been considered didactic. However, we have learned that not all teaching in history has been of this type. "Socrates, as we have noted, relied on the relationship between himself and his students to arrive at truths of human existence; he was, in Axelrod's sense, an 'evocative' teacher." Here, the teacher attempts to "elicit" from students "conclusions, probabilities, and hypotheses from a specific situation or facts." [22]

Whether we label the conflict as being between the science and the art of teaching or the didactic and evocative methods of teaching, teachers can undoubtedly employ a variety of methods to teach their students. Still, the debate in the United States during the nineteenth century concerning how best to teach had little impact on what was happening in most classrooms because most teachers had no specific training in teaching methods.[23]

In a study done during the 1896–1897 school year, the U.S. Commission of Education noted that "not more than one in five or one in six of the expected 50,000 new teaching jobs that would go open the following year would be filled by a normal school graduate." Even in Massachusetts, where normal schools began, only one-third of the teachers were educated in normal schools. Nationwide, somewhere between two-thirds and four-fifths of the teachers had no specific teacher training. Even as late as 1923, the majority of school boards did not require normal school training.[24]

Change in teacher training accelerated as the country moved into the progressive era at the beginning of the twentieth century. As a result of pressure from "education professionals—state, city, and county superintendents; faculty members at normal schools and teacher's colleges; editors of professional education journals," there was a movement to upgrade teacher-training schools and convert them into college-level programs, which included classes in "high school teaching, education administration, and educational research." In some states, normal schools were first transformed into community colleges, which offered a combination of liberal arts and professional classes.[25]

As normal schools sought to become colleges, there was significant conflict in the field of higher education. Established colleges and universities saw the possibility of creating schools of education, especially for secondary teachers. Normal school graduates increasingly found difficulty competing for jobs against college graduates. This was especially true for candidates seeking positions in high schools. As early as 1925, the state of Wisconsin passed legislation transforming normal schools into teachers colleges, which awarded bachelor degrees in teacher education.[26] During the next two decades, similar changes occurred in many states. In New York State, many normal schools were converted to state teachers colleges. These institutions would later add graduate programs. Eventually, larger teachers colleges, such as those located in Albany and Buffalo, New York, would become universities offering doctoral programs.

Normal schools did not give up their identities without a struggle. In 1923, a dean of a normal school in Cleveland, Ohio, "warned of those who were ready to turn teacher education over to universities." He said of them,

> They do not seem to understand that the professed interest of these institutions is, in large measure, sinister and is definitely related to campaigns for endowment or for the support of legislative appropriation bills. They overlook the fact that these institutions, generally

speaking, have no adequate equipment of the right sort, no program of studies and activities, and no professional staff for the training of teachers and that worse still, the cardinal education doctrines of the average academic professor includes such as that (1) he who knows a subject can teach it, and (2) the word "pedagogy" is an anathema and should be stricken out of all reputable dictionaries.[27]

Despite their efforts to survive, by the end of the 1920s, most normal schools had been taken over or were closed.

As the historical record of normal schools is considered, they are definitely given mixed reviews. As we have seen, the graduates never encompassed a majority of the teachers in public schools. A four-hundred-page report on normal schools prepared in 1921 was critical of most programs and recommended that teacher education take place at the college level. Among the other charges were that normal schools deliberately encouraged elementary teachers to use their normal school training as a "stepping stone" to high school teaching and school administration. Other studies suggested that normal schools de-emphasized the training of elementary teachers.[28]

While much of the public was still not ready to consider teachers as professionals at the end of the twentieth century, those who were able to become school administrators were increasingly given a level of respect in their communities. Furthermore, even in the early twentieth century, most teachers at the elementary level were women, but those in leadership positions in almost every school were men.[29]

The new programs in education at colleges and universities were slow to earn the respect of the professors and administrators in the more established disciplines. The early instructors in education programs often were experienced public school teachers who lacked advanced degrees. Their classes typically relied on their teaching experiences, and the curricula lacked significant emphasis on what some were calling "the science of education." This prejudice against education classes and departments has never totally dissipated. For many in the higher education community, education is viewed as a less-than-legitimate academic discipline.[30]

As four-year teacher education programs began to evolve, the most controversial issue was and remains the proper balance among liberal arts classes, education courses, and classroom experiences. As early as 1904, John Dewey shared his opinions on the essential aspects of an effective teacher preparation program. For this young professor, the important principles in establishing such a program were as follows:

- "The teacher candidate should have scholastic attainments."
- "The teacher candidate should have a period of observation to facilitate the teacher candidate's ability to perceive psychological development and reflect on the educational program of a school as a whole."

- "The teacher candidate should 'assist' the regular teacher to transcend theoretical and psychological insight with practical management techniques."
- "The teacher candidate should practice teach in a regular school (not a model school). The candidate should be responsible for the consecutive development of a subject field. Depth in one field vs. practice in a number of subjects is desired."
- "The teacher should have a period of probationary teaching to weed out persons unfit for the profession."[31]

While Dewey and other progressive educators were attempting to effect the teacher's role in the classroom, the institutions preparing teachers were undergoing a transformation. By the beginning of World War II, a majority of colleges were establishing departments of teacher education. Because so many students were seeking careers in education, such departments were often profitable, and some critics called them "cash cows," charging that there was inadequate financial support for these programs. Although the trend to prepare teachers in four-year colleges or universities did not catch on until the twentieth century, it actually started much earlier. In 1832, New York University created an education department as part of its college. Fifty-one years later, the University of Iowa had a chair for didactics (education), and by the turn of the century, many colleges had professors of pedagogy, even though, in some cases, the departments consisted of only one professor.[32]

The effort to create such a position at Columbia University was voted down by the trustees, but as a compromise, lectures on the subject were allowed on Sunday mornings. The issue at Columbia and other universities was that teaching was a form of vocationalism that, for many university professors, was not the major mission of the college. For them, the mission was to provide a liberal arts education to their students.[33]

It is important to note that the early attempts to infuse teacher education into four-year colleges and universities saw only limited success. Because only 4 percent of the college-age population attended college in 1900, it is certain that, at least when the century began, few students were gaining college training. The first programs specialized in preparing high school teachers and emphasized more advanced classes in the subject matter that the students would be teaching.

By 1915, a majority of the colleges were also offering education courses as a part of their curricula. These classes included testing and measurement, educational philosophy, and even some training in educational research. Some questioned the value of such courses, however. One graduate was quoted as saying, "'I could talk about [influential psychiatrist] Carl Jung, scaffolding, cooperative learning groups, [and] the advantages of constructivism,' but had no idea what to do, 'when Johnny goes nuts in the back of the class, or when Lisa comes in abused, or when Sue hasn't eaten in three days.'"[34] Such a quotation would not be a surprise in any era.

One of the chief challenges in creating a highly effective teacher education program is the need to develop some form of correlation between the liberal arts portion of the student's education and the professional education classes, including the time spent in classroom observation and student teaching. Because subject matter teachers were not frequently part of the education department, there was too often little or no collaboration with it. As a result, liberal arts faculty members felt minimal responsibility for shaping students into teachers.

In smaller colleges, these students might well be taking their science courses with future doctors and nurses. Many college teachers are specialists who are excited about their personal academic interests and do not think about the fact that "the teaching profession is one that calls for far more than abstract knowledge." Some larger colleges did make the effort to bring liberal arts faculty into their departments of education and design courses with teachers in mind. Such an approach does stimulate faculty dialogue on how to best prepare future teachers.[35]

These conversations can lead to allowing elementary teachers to replace a required math class in calculus with a course entitled "Math for Elementary School Teachers." Of course, in some colleges, such a change could lead to a spirited debate, as the math department might lose calculus students, which could reduce enrollment and endanger a faculty member's job. In any case, such discussions will continue as colleges attempt to determine what type of academic preparation is best for future elementary teachers. Furthermore, a future high school math teacher might gain more from a college calculus course if it were taught by an instructor who was sensitive to the importance of modeling effective teaching techniques.

Other problems arose as teacher education programs were infused into major universities. For example, in some institutions, departments of education had offices and classrooms spread all over campus. While law schools and medical schools were housed in their own buildings, many education programs had no such luxury. Even the administrators of education departments often had priorities other than the new teacher education curriculums.[36]

When Columbia University established the New York College of Education for the training of teachers in 1887, it did so with "great expectation for a new era." The program officially became part of Columbia University in 1892 and was renamed Teachers College. The merger has been described as encompassing "the widest street in the world": "120th Street in New York City—with Teachers College on one side and the rest of Columbia University on the other."[37]

Eventually, Columbia Teachers College emerged as one of the most prestigious education programs in the nation. In large part, it was the presence of John Dewey on the faculty that helped to create this reputation. Other outstanding programs were created at the University of California at Berkley and the University of Michigan. These schools were established as professional preparation programs and "gained respect and recognition outside their settings, but little within." Especially for professors working in these universities, the education departments were "commonly looked down upon as unwanted sisters—siblings who, if they did not actually besmirch the family name, were nonetheless to be disavowed." Some also thought that "scholars in the arts and sciences who taught without the benefit of training perceived the emergence of pedagogical science as a kind of insult—a put-down to their self-acquired art."[38]

The problems of teacher-training institutions have become even more complex in the late-twentieth and early-twenty-first centuries. As states have attempted to improve the education of future teachers, new demands have been placed on these programs. States such as New York have required that within five years, new teachers have an appropriate master's degree to maintain their certifications. Other states have added graduate school requirements as well, which has started a major debate over when education courses should be offered. Some colleges have argued that future teachers should first gain bachelor degrees in liberal arts and then complete graduate programs for teaching.

Others have argued that future teachers need to begin their preparation as college freshmen and have opportunities to observe and participate in classrooms during every year of their undergraduate programs. Along with the debate over the placement of education courses and the role of graduate work, states have placed another requirement on future teachers. Especially in recent years, certification has required students to pass tests in subject matter and pedagogy and, more recently, in the area of special education. Because teacher education programs are often judged by the success of their students on these examinations, they have entered the category of "high-stakes testing" for their programs. As a result, the tests can greatly affect the curriculum being taught in teacher education programs.

In an attempt to ensure the quality of teacher education programs, a process known as *accreditation* has emerged. A program was devised as early as 1950, and in 1954 the accrediting agency known as the National Council for the Accreditation of Teacher Education came to be. A rival organization emerged in the 1990s called the Teacher Education Accreditation Council, and between the two organizations, most teacher education programs have sought to be accredited.[39] Along with state regulations, these accrediting agencies have significant power in determining the type of teacher education programs that are offered.

Since there currently seems to be a national consensus that providing excellent teachers in every classroom is perhaps the most important factor in any attempt to improve our schools, public interest in teacher education has never been higher. Add to this the infusion of the Common Core curriculum as the basis of what is to be taught in language arts and math in forty-six states, and we see that teacher education programs are experiencing extraordinary challenges. Along with the Common Core initiative, the Race to the Top program of the federal government has caused states receiving grants to create more effective methods for evaluating teachers. Included in these systems is the use of student test results as one factor in determining a teacher's effectiveness.

These trends must all be addressed in our teacher education programs. Within the teacher education ranks, there is a lack of agreement on the directions that our country is taking in the field of education. There are those who feel that by emphasizing testing and common objectives, we are creating a system that severely limits teacher creativity and stifles what has been considered the "art" aspect of teaching. Others point out that the status quo of our educational system cannot be allowed to continue unchanged and that reforms such as the Common Core standards and stricter teacher evaluations are the best way of mending the system.

Even if we are moving in the right direction, the current initiatives cannot succeed unless the teacher education programs in this country are committed to these reforms. The sentiments expressed in *The Education of Teachers*, written in 1960, continue to be a realistic description of our teacher education programs. For these authors, our education schools

> are not all bad—not nearly so bad as the public and many educators have been led to believe. Extreme examples to sustain almost any preconceived viewpoint can be found in our system of mass education, if one searches long enough for them. In short, the situation is neither as good nor as bad as the pros or the cons would have it. But, the undeniable fact remains that it is not as good as it ought to be. Great improvements are necessary all along the line, and the need for action is urgent.[40]

As we look to the future and to the question of what our teaching methods should be, the role of teacher education programs cannot be ignored. Although the first teacher colleges emerged in the nineteenth century, there would be significant changes in both the colleges and the public schools of the twentieth century that would greatly influence teaching in America.

NOTES

1. K. E. Melder, "Woman's High Calling: The Teaching Profession in America, 1830–1860," *American Studies* 13 (fall 1972): 19–32.

2. John I. Goodlad, Roger Soder, and Kenneth A. Sirotnix, eds., *Places Where Teachers Are Taught* (San Francisco: Jossey-Bass, 1990), 139.

3. Goodlad, Soder, and Sirotnix, *Places Where Teachers Are Taught*.

4. *Common School Journal* 6 (September 2, 1844): 267.

5. *Common School Journal*, 267.

6. Goodlad, Soder, and Sirotnix, *Places Where Teachers Are Taught*, 134.

7. William E. Drake, *The American School in Transition* (Englewood Cliffs, NJ: Prentice Hall, 1955), 379.

8. Arthur M. Cohen and Carrie B. Kisker, *The Shaping of American Higher Education*, 2nd ed. (San Francisco: Jossey-Bass), 151.

9. George S. Morrison, *Teaching in America*, 4th ed. (Boston: Pearson Education, 2006), 326.

10. Karen Cheek, "The Normal School," http://www3.nd.edu/~rbarger/www7/normal.html.

11. Charles A. Harper, *A Century of Public Education* (Washington, DC: Hugh Birch–Horace Mann Fund for the American Association of Teachers Colleges, 1939), 47.

12. Harper, *A Century of Public Education*, 47.

13. Sol Cohen, ed., *Education in the United States: A Documentary History* (New York: Random House, 1974), 1780–1781.

14. Cohen, *Education in the United States*, 1780–1781.

15. Cohen, *Education in the United States*, 1781.

16. J. L. Meader, *Normal School Education in Connecticut* (New York: Teachers College, 1928), 69.

17. Meader, *Normal School Education in Connecticut*, 18.

18. David Diener, "The Intellectual Climate of the Late Nineteenth Century and the Fate of American Normal Schools," *American Educational History Journal* 35, no. 1 (2008): 67.

19. Diener, "The Intellectual Climate," 69.

20. Diener, "The Intellectual Climate," 69–70.

21. James W. Guthrie, ed., *Encyclopedia of Education*, vol. 7, 2nd ed. (New York: McMillan Reference, 2003), 2438.

22. Diener, "The Intellectual Climate," 2438.

23. James W. Fraser, *Preparing America's Teachers: A History* (New York: Teachers College, 2007), 131.

24. Fraser, *Preparing America's Teachers*, 131.

25. Donald Warren, ed., *American Teachers: Histories of a Profession at Work* (New York: Macmillan, 1989), 229.

26. Warren, *American Teachers*, 230.

27. Ambrose L. Suhrie, "The Teachers College as a Professional School," *Indiana State and Normal School* 17 (December 1923): 77.

28. Suhrie, "The Teachers College," 233.

29. Suhrie, "The Teachers College," 233.

30. G. K. Hodenfield and T. M. Stinnett, *The Education of Teachers* (Englewood Cliffs, NJ: Prentice Hall, 1961), 4.

31. Johanna Lemlech and Merl B. Marx, *The American Teacher, 1776–1996* (Bloomington, IN: Phi Delta Kappa Educational Foundation, 1976), 24.

32. John Pulliam and James J. Van Patten, *History of Education in America*, 9th ed. (Upper Saddle River, NJ: Pearson, 2007), 184.

33. Pulliam and Van Patten, *History of Education in America*, 184.

34. A. Levine, "Educating School Teachers" (2006), http://www.eduschool.org/pdf/Educating_Teachers_Report.pdf.

35. Robert A. Levin, *Educating Elementary School Teachers* (New York: University Press of America, 1994), 45.

36. John I. Goodlad, *Teachers for Our Nation's Schools* (San Francisco: Jossey-Bass, 1990), 73.

37. Goodlad, *Teachers for our Nation's Schools*, 74.

38. Goodlad, *Teachers for our Nation's Schools*, 74.

39. Guthrie, *Encyclopedia of Education*, 2442.
40. Hodenfield and Stinnett, *The Education of Teachers*, 150.

EIGHT

Teaching in the Last Half of the Twentieth Century

The teaching taking place in schools in the United States during the twentieth century was affected by a number of events and social trends. Although there have undoubtedly been changes in teaching styles, some argue that if you visited a high school English or social studies classroom at the beginning of the twenty-first century, you might see a lesson resembling one that was taught at the beginning of the twentieth century. Others point to numerous differences. As we have seen, some of the changes were effected by the impact of the progressive education movement, which was especially influential at the beginning of the twentieth century.

While the influence of progressive theory was strong in only some schools, it did influence, to a degree, how teaching occurred in almost every classroom. The notion that teachers must do more than provide information to their students has been accepted as a truism in our society. In most classrooms, teachers have adopted a variety of learning activities and methods. Many teachers have come to consider themselves as facilitators of student learning, but as we shall see, some current teachers have recently become frustrated by the limitations brought on by the need to "teach to the test."

At the same time, the impact of progressive theory has, admittedly, ebbed and flowed since its introduction. At the beginning of the century, the call for a change in teaching methods was coming not only from such philosophers as John Dewey but also from popular writers, whom President Theodore Roosevelt labeled "muckrakers." In his book *How the Other Half Lives*, Jacob Riis was perhaps overly optimistic when he wrote, "Do you see how the whole battle of the slum is fought out in and around the public school?" If we can reform public schools, "the battle with the slum will be over." Jane Addams, an influential social worker and friend of John Dewey, also called for change in how students were taught when she wrote, "We are impatient with the schools which lay all stress on reading and writing, suspecting them to rest on the assumption that all knowledge and interest must be brought to the children through the medium of books. Such an assumption fails to give the child any clue to the life about him, or any power to usefully or intelligently connect himself with it."[1]

By the 1920s, model progressive private schools such as Dalton and Walden were established in New York City, along with so-called laboratory schools at Columbia University and Ohio State University. Schools utilizing progressive theory also spread to public schools in such places as Shaker Heights, Ohio; Pasadena, California; and Denver, Colorado. Each of these schools adopted its own progressive methods, but all tended to focus on what was labeled *child-centered learning*.[2] The influence of Maria Montessori also began to emerge during this period.

With the support of Piaget and others, there were already a hundred Montessori schools in the United States by 1915. The movement declined after World War I, only to emerge again in the United States during the 1990s. While it is difficult to give an exact number, there are currently more than five thousand Montessori schools in the United States. All but about a hundred are private tuition schools, which cater to more affluent and perhaps liberal families. Tuition costs vary greatly and could be as much as $11,000 a year, while the current average might be closer to $4,000.[3]

An organization made up of those espousing progressive education, called the Progressive Education Association, existed from 1902 to 1955. During the 1930s, the group sponsored the eight-year study to compare progressive education teaching methods with traditional teaching methods. Author Alfie Kohn has written about this study:

> More than 1,500 students over four years were compared to an equal number of carefully matched students at conventional schools. The result: when they got to college, the experimental students did just as well as, and often better than, their traditionally educated counterparts on all counts: grades, extracurricular participation, and drop-out rate as well as on measures of such things as intellectual curiosity and resourcefulness. And here's the kicker: "the further a school departed from the traditional college preparatory program, the better was the record of its graduates."[4]

The results of this study had little impact on the teaching methods in public schools, and by 1940, the influence of progressive education had significantly declined in our public schools.[5] In 1952, a discouraged John Dewey wrote in *TIME Magazine* that the changes brought about by the progressive education movement "were minimal." He did suggest that the movement had made many teachers more aware of child development and less likely to rely on "education by fear and repression."[6]

Five years after this article was written, an event occurred that would significantly influence thought in the United States about what was happening in our schools. With the surprise launching of the Russian satellite *Sputnik* into space, many Americans began to question their "previously cozy assumptions about their nation's technological and educational superiority."[7]

Politicians at the national and state levels reacted quickly to what was seen as weakness in our educational system. Vast amounts of money were spent to provide a boost to our school science and math programs. Money was used to revise curriculums in biology, chemistry, physics, and math classes. In doing so, there was a new emphasis given to laboratory learning. Funds were also allotted for additional training for teachers in these fields. Looking back on these initiatives, the former assistant secretary for vocational education concluded that much of the reaction to *Sputnik* was "elitist," as it focused attention solely on students taking advanced science and math courses and ignored the many who were engaged in vocational training.[8]

For progressives, the impact of *Sputnik* and other social trends of the period made the decade of the 1950s, in the words of Diane Ravitch, "a horrible decade for progressive education." The conflict between those supporting traditional education and progressivism became nasty and personal. The progressives sometimes labeled their critics "a motley assortment of 'chronic tax conservationists,' 'congenital reactionaries,' 'witch hunters,' 'superior patriots,' 'dogma peddlers,' 'race haters,' and . . . 'academic conservatives.'"[9]

Yet, the author of the best-selling book *Educational Wastelands*, Arthur Bestor, wrote that the progressive initiatives had "set forth purposes of education so trivial as to forfeit the respect of thoughtful men by deliberately divorcing the schools from the disciplines of science and scholarship." This author and others called for a return to curriculums that were "systematic and sequential" and would encourage "systematic thinking." Bestor later became one of the founders of the Council on Basic Education.[10] For him, schools were overly concerned with the personal problems of adolescence and, as a result, were failing in their primary goal, which was the intellectual development of its students.[11]

A second influential critic was Admiral Hyman Rickover, who tied the outcome of the Cold War with Russia with the need for education reform in the United States. He was an advocate of the "back to basics" movement, which he stated involved "perspiration and not play or social activities." A question that he asked in his 1956 book *Education and Freedom* was "why Johnny could not read while Ivan could." The solution for Rickover was to worry less about "life adjustment" and return to an emphasis on science and math.[12] Even in best-selling novels of the period involving teaching, writers such as Frances Gray Patton in her book *Good Morning, Miss Dove* and James Hilton in his book *Goodbye, Mr. Chips* praised the traditional teaching methods of the main characters.[13]

Teaching methods during this period were also affected by events throughout the United States. What became known as the *civil rights movement* was given a major boost with the 1954 decision made in *Brown v. Topeka, Kansas*. This case began the forced racial integration of our public schools. Especially in the South, classrooms with both black students and white students presented new challenges for teachers as they contended with a culture that remained hostile toward integration. As black families moved into Northern cities, a trend began that now finds black and Hispanic children to be in the majority in most of our urban schools.

One result of this diversification of classrooms was the impetus to introduce what was called *multicultural education*. The idea was that we should be celebrating racial and gender diversity in our schools. This trend influenced the literature choices of teachers, as they were encouraged to ensure that black and female authors were included in their curricula. Music teachers were asked to introduce their students to composers other than those from the classical European tradition. History books were revised to ensure that they included the contributions of women, Native Americans, and immigrants. Even with this trend, there was not unanimous support.

Some critics worried that multiculturalism would weaken the school's historical mission of being a "melting pot" for the diverse student bodies represented in schools. Some writers argued that all American children should be introduced to a common American culture to help them become assimilated into our society. They felt that multicultural projects such as Black History Month would only interfere with the goal of assimilation.

Racial tensions and other trends and events made the 1960s and early 1970s different from the 1950s. The killing of John F. Kennedy in 1963 and, later in the decade, the assassinations of Martin Luther King Jr. and Robert Kennedy created uneasiness in the American people. Added to this were the protests in schools and colleges over our nation's involvement in the Vietnam War. There was a general feeling, especially among many young people, that the nation was headed in the wrong direction.

This youthful rebellion did not touch all students, but it did affect most schools. Enough young people were unhappy that the press began to talk about a "generation gap" between youth and adults. For some, this gap extended to parents. Bob Dylan would include this idea in his song "The Times, They Are A-Changin."[14]

Students in high schools were involved in their own personal rebellions. Some boys let their hair grow long; girls insisted on being able to wear slacks or jeans rather than skirts to school. Among many students, the "back to basic" trends in the curriculum during the 1950s were not relevant. Some schools reacted to this student dissatisfaction by introducing a variety of electives and miniclasses on current issues. Classes such as "Problems of Democracy" or "The Humanities" were an attempt to capture the interest of high school students. On the practical side, driver education was introduced, in part, to help allow students to drive at night at an earlier age. Some schools even accommodated their student smokers by giving them a lounge in which to smoke during their free periods.

Extracurricular activities were expanded to include new topics reflecting current student interests. Still, many teenagers remained dissatisfied with schools, and it was not unusual to read about student demonstrations, not only at the college level, but in high schools. Male teachers attempting to adjust to this unrest often chose to stop wearing shirts and ties in their classrooms to help create a more informal setting.

During most of the 1960s, the Democratic Party was in the majority in Washington. Along with civil rights laws to help minorities, President Lyndon Johnson launched his War on Poverty. A significant aspect of these legislative initiatives was a serious attempt to help improve the education of poor children especially. Johnson introduced Head Start, a comprehensive program designed to provide students from impoverished families with a preschool experience that would offer not only classes but also health services and parental involvement. The most important federal legislation regarding education during the period was the 1965 passage of the Elementary-Secondary Education Act. For the first time, large amounts of federal aid were provided to local school districts to finance remedial programs in reading and mathematics.

The allotment of money that a district would receive was dependent on the number of poor children attending school in the district. Districts were able to hire remedial teachers, and elementary teachers especially found themselves being required to allow certain students to be pulled out of their classrooms for remedial reading or mathematics. This law was to be reauthorized every five years, and during the process of the reauthorization in 2001, it was dramatically revised and given the name No Child Left Behind.

It was also during this period that the teaching profession became more militant. For decades, school administrators and teachers together made up the membership of the National Education Association, which provided professional publications for its members and, at the state and federal levels, lobbied for educational legislation beneficial to teachers. Not thought of as a union, the organization was often dominated by school administrators. Although the first actual teachers union was founded in Chicago at the beginning of the twentieth century, it was not until 1944 that any local union "exercised any local control over a school system."

This occurred when the union in Cicero, Illinois, signed a collective bargaining contract with its Board of Education. Three years later, the American Federation of Labor affiliate in Buffalo, New York, carried out the first strike by teachers. The growth in membership of the American Federation of Teachers prompted the National Education Association to change the nature of its organization, and it too began to utilize union tactics, including picketing and even strikes. With this change, administrators were no longer accepted as members of the National Education Association.

The American Federation of Teachers gained additional power, as it became part of the national union alliance known as the American Federation of Labor, which would merge with the Congress of Industrial Organizations to create a national union among trade and industrial unions. While the National Education Association remains the largest teacher labor organization, with the American Federation of Teachers, teachers unions generally have become a major force in effecting education decisions.

The union movement has also influenced how teachers perceive their jobs, as collective bargaining now affects not only their salaries and fringe benefits but also such issues as school calendars and planning time. In many communities, unions have influenced the public's feelings about teachers. This has been especially true in districts where teachers have resorted to picketing or strikes. The once-complacent, hard-working public servant is seen by some as just another union member who is primarily concerned with improving one's wages and working conditions. In recent years, teachers have been caught between what seem like conflicting goals. On one hand, they desire to be considered professionals and to be compared with doctors and lawyers, while on the other, they are politically aligned with blue-collar unions. This dilemma has yet to be resolved, even in the twenty-first century.

The unrest of the sixties brought new support for a more progressive approach to teaching. In 1964, author John Holt argued,

> Most children in school fail. . . . They fail because they are afraid, bored, and confused . . . bored because the things they are given and told to do in school are so trivial, so dull, and make such limited and narrow demands on the wide spectrum of their intelligence, capabilities, and talents. . . . Schools should be a place where children learn what they want to know, instead of what we think they ought to know. [15]

Another spokesman of what became "the new left," Paul Goodman, called for dramatic changes in our schools, suggesting,

> The passions that followed *Sputnik* and the college panic divided us between those who wanted to make education a more efficient training instrument for the Cold War and middle-management, and those who resisted because the pap of life adjustment was more comfortable than

intellectual rigor. The new critics have reminded us—sometimes, albeit, with too much wail—that relevant education has little to do with either, and that if it does not deal with the humanity of its students, it is not dealing with anything.[16]

This new rebellion led to a number of educational experiments in the 1960s. They included trends to build public schools without walls to break down the pattern of isolating teachers involved in only their own academic disciplines. Team teaching was also introduced as a practice that encouraged teachers at a grade level to work together in providing a more interdisciplinary approach to learning. Another trend was called *modular scheduling*, and it broke class times into various lengths to escape the monotony of forty-minute periods and offer flexibility to teachers. A similar approach emerged decades later called *block scheduling*.

There were also experiments that adopted much more radical changes. In England, at the Summerhill School, the goal was to have children "grow to be loving and happy adults." To achieve this objective, "children were given complete freedom to attend or not attend classes and were allowed to participate in the operation of the school."[17] The idea even spread to the United States, where in Minneapolis, Minnesota, schools were established using the Summerhill philosophy.[18]

Another significant trend that began in the 1960s was the idea of giving parents and students their choice of public school. So-called magnet schools were created primarily in cities. While they had to conform to the same curricula and regulations as the other public schools in the district, these schools had specific academic focuses. For example, a magnet school might be created for students interested in the arts. The curriculum in such a school included a significant number of specialized electives related to music or art. Such a school also had more performing groups than other public schools.

A magnet school could also focus on science or be an honors program where students from other city public schools would have to compete for acceptance. It was hoped that these schools would also break down the racial segregation emerging in cities as a result of the neighborhood approach to assigning school attendance.

At the elementary level, there was a movement to transform the way that students were taught to read. Called *whole language*, it sought to reduce the use of the traditional reliance on the basal reading series, along with the accompanying workbooks. The idea was to substitute the best children's literature and use it as the basis for teaching reading and writing. In addition, word identification relied on context clues, and the use of phonics was de-emphasized. Elementary faculties and administrators became embroiled in fierce debates over the best way to teach reading. Math curriculum did not escape controversy, as the approach known as *new math* was introduced in many schools.

Perhaps the most popular movement in the organization of schools began when middle schools emerged during the 1960s. Before this, most large school districts had patterns that placed K–6 students in elementary schools, grades 7–9 in junior high schools, and grades 10–12 in high schools. Some educators felt that junior high schools were mainly "mini–high schools" that were failing to provide students with adequate transitions between elementary programs (where students worked with a single teacher for most of the day) to high schools (where they moved to different teachers every forty-five minutes).

Because children between the ages of eleven and thirteen are often experiencing difficult periods in their adolescence, it was thought that schools that focused on the characteristics of this age level would better help them to succeed in the more competitive high school environment. In theory, such schools would have teachers working in teams and would provide students with adult mentors and guidance counselors, career exploration, and additional parental involvement.[19] Teaching methods would include more hands-on activities; even extracurricular programs would be different from those at the high school.

Instead of school dances, there might be "activity nights" where students played games. The athletic programs would offer every student a chance to participate in games, and the emphasis would be on the experience rather than on winning. The middle school movement spread to smaller districts as well, as rural schools chose to break up their grade 7–12 programs and create separate middle schools. Some states reacted to the middle school trend by requiring future teachers to take classes in middle school theory. New York State would go further and require a separate certification for middle school teachers.

Still, another major movement greatly affected how some children were taught. The federal government sought to ensure that those students in need of special education were provided equal opportunities to succeed in school. Beginning in 1973 with a law entitled the Rehabilitation Act, which prohibited "discrimination by failure to provide access and reasonable facilities for people with disabilities," a series of laws that sought to protect the educational rights of all children were passed. The primary legislation that forced schools to act was public law 94-142, passed by Congress in 1975.[20]

This law created the need for school districts to establish committees to consider all referrals for all students who might be in need of special education. Those disabilities that were considered deserving of special attention were as follows:

- Mental retardation
- Hearing impairment, including deafness
- Speech or language impairment
- Visual impairment

- Serious emotional disturbance
- An orthopedic impairment
- Autism
- Traumatic brain injury
- A specific learning disability
- Deaf-blindness
- Multiple disabilities[21]

Students in any of these categories could be assigned special services and individualized education plans, which outline specific annual goals and objectives for each student. The law also required that these special education students be placed in the "least restrictive environment," interpreted to mean "in a classroom most like a regular classroom in which the student could succeed." Initially, in many states and districts, the law was interpreted to allow special education students to be placed in self-contained classes with other students with similar disabilities.

Gradually, the least restrictive environment clause led parents to seek more inclusive placements. For some, this meant pullout mainstreaming opportunities for certain subjects, but for others, it meant resource room placement or placement in a regular classroom with a special education aide. Eventually, approximately 13 percent of the students in the United States were identified as being in need of special education services, which could include speech therapy, counseling, physical or occupational therapy, or, in some cases, music therapy.

The law was further strengthened in 1990 with the passage of the Individuals with Disabilities Education Act and the education amendments of 1997. As a result of these laws, the provisions of public law 94–142 were extended to citizens from the ages of two to twenty-one years.[22] The results of the special education laws and other new laws greatly affected teaching in our schools. Because of the inclusion movement—which forced schools to place special education students in the classroom environment most like that of non–special education students—teachers could have a student with an IQ of 65 in the same class with an intellectually gifted student with an IQ more than 130. As a result, teachers are now expected to "differentiate" their instruction methods to meet the academic needs of very different students. This has led schools into debates about academic grouping or ability grouping, which many critics see as a form of discrimination.

To avoid such practices, the same required tests are now mandated for almost every student, including those receiving special education services. If all students are taking the same test, academic grouping becomes less likely. This has led proponents of separate classes for gifted students to suggest that inclusion is detrimental to these more able children, as teachers must spend more time and effort in teaching the children with special needs in their classes.

Criticism of all the educational experiments of the 1960s and 1970s came to a head when Ronald Reagan's secretary of education, Terrell Bell, appointed a special commission called the National Commission on Excellence in Education to consider the status of education in the United States. The group was made up of businesspeople, college professors, representatives of teachers unions, and others. They spent a year studying special reports and holding hearings. The report that they finally submitted to the president was described by educational historian Diane Ravitch as "the most important educational reform document of the 20th century." It "captured the national attention, shaping the terms of the debate about schooling for a generation after its publication."[23]

The report was widely publicized in the United States, and its language was highly critical of our educational system. In fact, the economic problems facing the country were thought to be, in large part, a by-product of the poor education that our children were receiving. The argument was made that the failure to compete successfully in world markets resulted from a lack of qualified scientists and other workers. At this point in its history, the country was plagued by high unemployment, as many industries were leaving the country. The stirring words of the report did have an impact on the public's view of its schools. The following words were quoted in all the media:

> Our nation is at risk. Our once unchallenged preeminence in commerce, industry, science, and technological innovation is being overtaken by competitors throughout the world. . . . The educational foundations of our society are presently being eroded by a rising tide of mediocrity that threatens our very future as a Nation and a people. . . . If an unfriendly foreign power had attempted to impose on America the mediocre educational performance that exists today, we might well have viewed it as an act of war. As it stands, we have allowed this to happen to ourselves. . . . We have, in effect, been committing an act of unthinking, unilateral educational disarmament.[24]

A major emphasis in the recommendations called for a "back to basics" initiative. In addition, there was support for limiting the number of electives offered in high schools, increasing the amount of homework, raising teacher salaries, placing a greater emphasis on technology, creating curriculum standards, and improving the education of future teachers.[25]

As a result of the *Nation at Risk* report, hundreds of panels were formed at the local and state levels. Among the early results were the following:

- Forty states increased course requirements for graduation.
- Thirty-three states instituted testing for student promotion or graduation.
- Almost half the states passed legislation to increase qualifications, standards, and pay for teachers.

- Many states increased the length of the school day and/or school year.
- Most states passed laws that required teachers and students to demonstrate computer literacy.[26]

Perhaps one of the most important long-range impacts of the report was the beginning of the standards movement. Over the next several decades, states would attempt to write what students should know and be able to do in every subject. The *Nation at Risk* report sowed the seeds for the reform movements in education occurring in the twenty-first century. The most important of the initiatives were the changes brought about by the No Child Left Behind law, signed by President George W. Bush in 2002. Its effect on teaching in America has been profound.

NOTES

1. David B. Tyack, ed., *Turning Points in American Educational History* (Malthan, MA: Blaisdell, 1967), 318–19.

2. Myra Pollack Sadker and David Miller Sadker, *Teachers, Schools and Society*, 2nd ed. (New York: McGraw-Hill, 1991), 290.

3. William Hayes, *The Progressive Education Movement: Is it Still a Factor in Today's Schools?* (Lanham, MD: Rowman & Littlefield Education, 2006), 88–89.

4. Alfie Kohn, *The Schools Our Children Deserve* (Boston: Houghton Mifflin, 1999), 232.

5. David Tyack, Robert Lowe, and Elisabeth Hansot, *Public Schools in Hard Times* (Cambridge, MA: Harvard University Press, 1984), 155.

6. Joel Spring, *American Education* (Boston: McGraw-Hill, 2006), 269.

7. Sean Cavanagh, "Lessons Drawn from *Sputnik* 50 Years Later," *Education Week* 27, no. 5 (2007): 1, 13–14.

8. Cavanagh, "Lessons Drawn."

9. Lawrence A. Cremin, *The Transformation of the School* (New York: Knopf, 1964), 342–43.

10. L. Dean Webb, *The History of American Education* (Upper Saddle River, NJ: Pearson Prentice Hall, 2006), 263.

11. Allan C. Ornstein, *Pushing the Envelope, Critical Issues in Education* (Upper Saddle River, NJ: Merrill Prentice Hall, 2003), 84.

12. Ornstein, *Pushing the Envelope*, 84.

13. Hayes, *The Progressive Education Movement*, 38–39.

14. Bob Dylan, "The Times, They Are A-Changin'," *The Times, They Are A-Changin'* (Columbia Records, 1964).

15. Jack L. Nelson, Stuart B. Palonsky, and Mary Rose McCarthy, *Critical Issues in Education* (Boston: McGraw-Hill, 2004), 20.

16. Stan Dropkin, Harold Full, and Ernest Schwarcz, *Contemporary American Education* (London: Macmillan, 1970), 274.

17. Joel Spring, *The American School: 1642–1990* (New York: Longman, 1990), 367.

18. Spring, *The American School*, 368.

19. George S. Morrison, *Teaching in America* (Boston: Pearson, 2006), 93–94.

20. John D. Pulliam and James J. Van Patten, *History of Education in America*, 9th ed. (Upper Saddle River, NJ: Pearson, 2007), 320.

21. Spring, *The American School*, 92.

22. Pulliam and Van Patten, *History of Education in America*, 124.

23. Paul E. Peterson, ed., *Our Schools and Our Future: Are We Still at Risk?* (Stanford, CA: Hoover Institution Press, 2003), 25.

24. Diane Ravitch, ed., *The American Reader: Words That Moved a Nation* (New York: HarperCollins, 1991), 361.

25. William Hayes, *Are We Still a Nation at Risk Two Decades Later?* (Lanham, MD: Scarecrow Education, 2004), 25.

26. David Hill, "Fixing the System from the Top Down," *Teacher Magazine* (September/October 1989): 50–55.

II

Present

NINE

The Effects of No Child Left Behind on Teaching in America

As a result of legislation entitled the Improving American Schools Act under President Clinton in 1994, many recommendations of the *Nation at Risk* report were implemented. By the time that George W. Bush took office in 2001, forty-eight states had received approval from the federal Department of Education for their curriculum standards development processes. This law started the movement that, by the second decade of the twenty-first century, had resulted in what is known as the Common Core standards. Passage of the No Child Left Behind law in 2001 greatly magnified the role played by the federal government in how teaching would take place in American schools.

Looking back, it is surprising that the involvement of the federal government in public education should increase as a result of the leadership of a Republican president. Prior to the 2000 presidential election, Republican national platforms had called for less federal control of schools. For most conservatives, education was thought to be the responsibility of state and local governments. There is historical support for this point of view, as the U.S. Constitution does not delegate to either the president or the Congress specific power in governing schools. In addition, these conservatives argue that, historically, until the second half of the twentieth century, our schools had been controlled at the state and local levels.

Liberals, however, point to the fact that local control had led to a system where schools varied greatly in the opportunities they offered children. One of the major reasons for this is the reliance on property taxes as a major form of financial support. Property-rich suburban schools have been able to spend significantly more on their programs than most urban and poor rural districts. As a result, equality of educational opportunity for American children has been uneven at best. Because states and local communities have been unable or unwilling to provide a system that offers all children an opportunity to succeed, many liberals have concluded that the best way to solve the problem is to increase federal involvement.

In the 2000 presidential campaign, candidate Bush and his advisors made the decision to focus on the issue of improving schools. Even though calling for a more active federal role in education was contrary to the historical Republican philosophy, there were several reasons for the decision to raise the issue during the campaign. First of all, in the year 2000, one survey listed education as the number one issue facing our nation.[1] A second reason for emphasizing education was that Bush had focused on education as governor of Texas. During the campaign, he made a great show of pointing to how his programs had raised test scores. Some of the media accepted the idea that the governor's personal initiatives had created what was labeled as "the Texas miracle."[2]

While researchers would later seriously question the success of the Texas educational initiatives, for George Bush, the issue was one that he would use effectively in his campaign against Democrat Al Gore. The Republican platform during the campaign included support for the following school initiatives:

- Private school vouchers
- Phonics-based reading programs
- Character education
- Abstinence-only sex education
- State curriculum standards
- High-stakes testing[3]

As president, Bush wasted no time in seeking to keep his campaign promise to use the federal government to improve education in America.

A number of factors led to a relatively rapid passage of comprehensive legislation aimed at improving education. The timetable was favorable in that the reauthorization of the major federal legislation dealing with education was due to occur during President Bush's term. The Elementary Secondary Education Act was initially passed in 1965 as a part of President Lyndon Johnson's War on Poverty and had been reauthorized periodically since its passage. Congress was to again consider reauthorization in 2001.

Democrats in Congress, led by Senator Ted Kennedy, were seeking to dramatically increase federal spending on education. As a result of bipartisan efforts, Kennedy and other prominent Democrats, along with the president, were able to complete their work by January 2002. The final product included more than one thousand pages and was given the new name No Child Left Behind. The title of the legislation was most likely adopted from an article written by Marian Wright Edelman, the longtime president of a group called the Children's Defense Fund. In her article, Edelman had written, "When Jesus Christ invited little children to come unto Him, He did not invite only rich, middle-class, white male children without disabilities from two-parent families or our own children to come. He welcomed all children."[4]

Hers was only one voice urging efforts to ensure that education was being offered equally to all students. Other writers, such as Jonathon Kozol, whose book *Savage Inequalities* was on the best-seller list, brought to the nation's attention the great gaps in educational achievement of different groups in our population. The legislation that was passed with significant bipartisan support in both houses of Congress was an attempt by our national leadership to address the inequalities present in the system.

It is not the purpose here to summarize the provisions of this massive law but to suggest that it has had an important effect on teaching in our schools. No one can argue with the president's description of the purpose of No Child Left Behind, which was to ensure that "every child in every school must be performing at grade level in the basic subjects that are key to all learning: reading, and math."[5] Among the most important provisions of the law was the requirement that each state develop curriculum standards and tests in the fields of language arts and math in grades 3–8. In addition, tests must be given in science at the elementary, middle, and high school levels. The focus on these three subjects was a continuation of the "back to basics" emphasis urged in the *Nation at Risk* report.

To ensure that states take the testing and other requirements of the law seriously, the legislation also requires that school districts and states make annual school report cards public. In a significant attempt to ensure that no child would be left behind, the results of the tests had to include a breakdown based on eight subgroups: the mandated categories include white, black, Hispanic, American Indian, and Asian or Pacific Islander; also, there must be separate reporting for students eligible for free or reduced-price lunches, those with limited English proficiency, and those qualifying for special education services.[6]

Test results were to be measured using a complex system which attempts to measure adequate yearly progress (AYP). Schools not meeting AYP in any subcategory would be dealt with in the following way:

- Low-performing schools that do not improve in two years will receive technical assistance from the school district for school improvement.
- After three years of no improvement, the school will be required to offer parents supplemental educational services, including private tutoring.
- After four years of no school improvement, the district must replace some staff and adopt a new curriculum.

- After five years of no school improvement, the school would be completely reorganized with an alternative governance structure, such as reopening as a charter school.[7]

Such dire consequences for schools failing to meet their AYP requirements have undoubtedly affected teachers and what is taking place in classrooms. This is especially true in grades 3–8, where most of the required tests are given. As a result of the law, the term *high-stakes testing* has become frequently cited as a problem for schools and teachers. Test results have taken on extra importance not only for teachers but for students as well. Some children become very concerned that the test results could affect their promotion to the next grade level. Parents worry not only about this but also about how poor tests could affect their children's future. Board of Education members can see the results as a measure of their effectiveness. Finally, school administrators are being judged on how well their students are doing and whether scores are rising or declining.

One result of the emphasis on testing has been a reduction in the amount of classroom time spent on subjects which do not mandate testing. The Center on Educational Policy conducted a survey that found that "since the passage of the federal law, 71 percent of the nation's 15,000 school districts had reduced the hours of instructional time spent on history, music, and other subjects to open more time for reading and math."[8] Perhaps hardest hit has been the area of social studies, where a spokesman for the National Council for Social Studies was quoted as saying, "The worst thing that has ever happened to social studies has been the No Child Left Behind law."[9] There is also the issue of time being spent in teaching test-taking skills to students.

Because the tests are mandated for almost all students, other critics have observed that attention being given to the at-risk students has caused schools and teachers to neglect gifted students, who have no trouble passing the tests. Proponents of the arts are upset, as the time being allotted for music and art classes has been reduced in many schools. At a time when childhood obesity is at record levels, shorter or less frequent physical education classes have also been a by-product of the emphasis on testing in some districts.

Another prominent provision of the law requires that states ensure that there is a "highly qualified teacher" in every classroom. Many states have sought to meet this provision by requiring that schools employ only state-certified teachers. While this requirement has reduced the number of uncertified teachers, it also has led states to approve shortcut programs for state certification. These so-called alternative education programs have the goal of enticing individuals with strong academic backgrounds to enroll in shortened professional programs that allow them to be certified more quickly. This initiative, which includes the federal program

Teach for America, has not been universally applauded. A study done in 2007 concluded, "Entry standards are abysmally low: two-thirds of the programs surveyed accept half or more of their teacher applicants; one quarter accept virtually everyone who applies."[10]

Linda Darling-Hammond questions the alternative programs and suggests instead that the appropriate model for preparing teachers be one that is similar to the way that we prepare physicians. To do this, she suggests that the federal government subsidize schools in the same way that it now subsidizes teaching hospitals. She also favors a major scholarship program to recruit and retain excellent teachers, especially for high-need schools.[11]

The early results of the passage of the law saw some improvement in test scores and a shrinking of the gap between black and white students. In 2007, the federal education department published a report claiming, "No Child Left Behind is working." Not everyone agreed. Writing in the journal *Phi Delta Kappan*, Anne C. Lewis concluded, "No Child Left Behind, as a 'silver bullet' for education, 'is pretty much a dud.'"[12]

In any case, President Bush pointed to the law as being one of the major accomplishments of his first administration. Senator Kennedy, who had worked with the president to pass the legislation, was quickly critical of the fact that the administration was failing to recommend the increased funding that had been promised. The lack of money for carrying out the required mandates was undoubtedly affected by the cost of the war in Iraq. During the president's second term, criticisms grew to the point where the majority of those in education supported modifications of the law. In the 2008 presidential campaign, both Barack Obama and John McCain admitted that No Child Left Behind needed to be reworked.

As president, Obama sought to gain a comprehensive reauthorization bill, and even though the Senate education committee did approve of a major revision, it never reached the floor of the Senate. In the House of Representatives, after 2010, the wave of new Tea Party conservatives opposed any legislation that maintained a major role for the federal government in managing our schools. Frustration concerning the failure of Congress to act in September 2011 led the Obama administration to the introduction of a waiver program that would allow states that met certain conditions to be released from many of the No Child Left Behind requirements. In part, the program was devised to save schools and districts from their likely failure to meet the AYP goals established by the legislation. At the time of the introduction of the waivers, it was predicted that "more than 80 percent of the schools . . . would be labeled as failing" by the 2014 deadline set by the law.[13]

Although many states were anxious for waivers, they were forced to create plans that included a number of federally mandated initiatives that would greatly affect teachers and schools. Perhaps most important was the requirement that school districts create effective methods to evaluate teachers and principals. These new plans must include student achievement as measured by test scores as a significant factor in any evaluation system. In states where new methods have been adopted, there has been increasing pressure to teach to the test. This occurred at the same time that a national recession was causing many districts to lay off teachers, which in some cases led to larger class sizes.

In addition to the evaluation programs, to gain approval for a waiver, states were required to adopt "college- and career-ready standards."[14] Although not mandated, one way that this provision could be met was by state adoption of the Common Core standards. As of mid-2013, forty-seven states, the District of Columbia, Puerto Rico, and the Bureau of Indian Education had submitted requests for Elementary Secondary Education Act flexibility. Thirty-seven states as well as the District of Columbia had been approved.[15]

In June 2013, it appeared that Congress was finally beginning to make an effort to break the deadlock on the reauthorization of No Child Left Behind. Tom Harkin, chairperson of the education committee, introduced a 1,156-page bill that he suggested was meant to take "the federal government out of the business of micro-managing schools." Although the bill did receive some positive comments, there were concerns expressed by critics both conservative and liberal. Perhaps the most important opposition came from his fellow committee member Republican Lamar Alexander. A spokesman for Alexander described the Harkin bill as being "congested with federal mandates." Alexander offered a shorter reauthorization plan that his aide claimed would "get Washington out of the business of deciding whether schools and teachers are succeeding or failing."[16]

In the House of Representatives, John Kline, the chairperson of the House education committee, had a very different approach to reauthorization that would go even further than Senator Alexander's in reducing the role of the federal government.[17] Monty Neill, writing in the *Washington Post*, stated, "Unfortunately, neither house is going to eliminate the test-and-punish core of [No Child Left Behind]—even though the growing public demand for fundamental change is backed by volumes of research." For teachers and teaching, the important issue concerning reauthorization is the testing requirement and its use of student test results as a major criterion in the way that teachers are evaluated.[18]

The opposition from teachers appears to be growing. In June 2013, 20,000 teachers, parents, and students converged on the state capitol of New York in Albany to protest the current reforms.[19] On the national front, a new educational organization emerged to oppose many of the changes taking place. Along with calling for additional funding, another of the group's goals is to make student learning "engaging and relevant." To do this, the group wishes to "elevate educators' autonomy and support their efforts to reach every student." The organization includes a number of well-known educational leaders, such as Linda Darling-Hammond, Jonathon Kozol, Diane Ravitch, and Robert B. Reich, former U.S. secretary of labor. The group, called the Education Opportunity Network, is enlisting support from teachers, parents, and students in an attempt to form a coalition to influence the efforts of Congress as it seeks to reauthorize No Child Left Behind.

There is no question that No Child Left Behind and the Obama waiver program have greatly affected teaching in America. Another trend that has emerged at the same time is perhaps even more important in affecting what is happening in our classrooms. The Common Core curriculum is telling teachers what their objectives should be in language arts and mathematics.

NOTES

1. Patrick J. McGuinn, *No Child Left Behind and the Transformation of Federal Education Policy, 1965–2005* (Lawrence: University Press of Kansas, 2006), 149.

2. Harcourt Assessment, "History of the No Child Left Behind Act of 2001," http://www.harcoutassessment.com.

3. Ken Goodman, Patrick Shannon, Yetta Goodman, and Roger Rapoport, eds., *Saving Our Schools* (Berkeley, CA: RDR Books, 2004), 3.

4. Marian Wright Edelmen, "Standing Up for the World's Children: Leave No Child Behind," http://www.womenspeecharchive.org/women/profile/speech/index.cfm?ProfileID=117&SpeechID=487.

5. Mary E. Williams, ed., *Education, Opposing Viewpoints* (Detroit, MI: Thomson Gayle, 2005), 156.

6. Scott Franklin Abernathy, *No Child Left Behind and the Public Schools* (Ann Arbor: University of Michigan Press, 2007), 5.

7. Joel Spring, *American Education* (Boston: McGraw-Hill, 2006), 197.

8. Sam Dillon, "Schools Cut Back Subjects to Push Reading and Math," *New York Times*, March 26, 2006, http://www.nytimes.com/2006/03/26/education/26child.html.

9. Dillon, "Schools Cut Back Subjects."

10. Peter W. D. Wright, Pamela Darr Wright, and Suzanne Whitney Heath, *No Child Left Behind* (Hartfield, VA: Harbor House Law Press, 2004), 25–26.

11. Wright, Wright, and Heath, *No Child Left Behind*, 25–26.

12. Anne C. Lewis, "An Ammunition Dump," *Phi Delta Kappan*, December 2005, 260.

13. Jason Amos, "Obama Sets Timeline for NCLB Revamp," March 22, 2011, http://all4ed.org/articles/obama-sets-timeline-for-nclb-revamp-president-calls-on-congress-to-send-him-an-education-reform-bill-before-the-next-school-year-begins/.

14. Gene E. Hall, Linda F. Quinn, and Donna M. Gollnick, *Introduction to Teaching: Making a Difference in Student Learning* (Thousand Oaks, CA: Sage, 2014), 262.

15. Department of Education, "ESEA Flexibility," http://www2.ed.gov/policy/elsec/guid/esea-flexibility/index.html.

16. Motoko Rich, "Bill to Alter Bush-Era Education Law Gives States More Room," *New York Times*, June 4, 2013, http://www.nytimes.com/2013/06/05/education/harkin-schools-legislation.html.

17. Alyson Klein, "Senate Democrats to Unveil NCLB Reauthorization Bill," *Education Week*, June 4, 2013, http://blogs.edweek.org/edweek/campaign-k-12/2013/06/embargoed_do_not_publish.html.

18. Valerie Strauss, "Don't Expect Congress to End Test-and-Punish Core of NCLB," *Washington Post*, June 5, 2013, http://www.washingtonpost.com/blogs/answer-sheet/wp/2013/06/05/dont-expect-congress-to-end-test-and-punish-core-of-nclb.html.

19. "Albany Education Rally," *Daily News*, June 10, 2013, A2.

TEN

The Impact of the Common Core Curriculum on Teaching

The idea of curriculum standards is not new in the twenty-first century. To understand the significance of what are now called the *Common Core standards*, it is important to first understand something about their origin and the meaning of the term. For many who are not actively involved in the public schools, the word *standard* denotes something different from the way that it is now used in our schools. For example, a definition listed in *Webster's Dictionary* is "something set up and established by authority as a rule for the measure of quantity, weight, extent, value, or quality." Often, the term is used when we suggest that "something is not up to standard."

Today, educators are using the term in a different way. For them, the Common Core standards refer to what students at each grade level should know and be able to do in any subject. Secretary of education Arne Duncan sees the Common Core not as a curriculum; rather, his definitions of *standards* and *curriculum* are as follows:

> *Standards:* "learning standards, academic standards . . . the goals, typically set by states, for what students should know by a certain age."
>
> *Curriculum:* "what teachers teach to help students meet those standards. Curriculum is generally chosen at the district or even the school level—and in many cases individual teachers actually decide on the curriculum and classroom content."[1]

The beginning of the effort to articulate state curriculum standards occurred as a result of the *Nation at Risk* report and was further stimulated by No Child Left Behind. In creating No Child Left Behind, Congress and the president agreed that it should be the responsibility of each state

95

to draw up individual curriculum standards. During the debate leading up to the final passage, many Democrats favored national curriculum standards, but the Republicans insisted that it was the role of state governments. The idea of pursuing national standards arose again in 1996 at the National Education Summit, which included a group of governors, representatives of both political parties, and a number of corporate leaders. As a result of this meeting, an organization entitled Achieve was created. Its purpose was to consider the development of curriculum standards that could be used in every state.[2]

This organization was formed as a partnership sponsored by the National Governors Association and the Council of Chief School Officers. The primary initiative of this group was to establish a commission that included curriculum experts as well as some teachers and school administrators. Working together, they were responsible for creating the Common Core standards for language arts and mathematics.[3] Currently, Common Core curriculums are being created in other subjects, and by the summer of 2013, a number of states had already accepted the Common Core in the field of science.

Even though the original project included only language arts and math, the goals of the curriculum do include other subjects. For example, at the high school level, there is a requirement that "reading, writing, speaking and listening, and language are also translated to literacy standards in history and social studies, science, and technical subjects. The expectation is that students will develop literacy skills specific to these subject areas in addition to what they learn in their language arts classes." The overall goals of the Common Core are as follows:

- "to specify key knowledge and skills in a format that makes it clear what teachers and assessments need to focus on";
- "to raise the achievement bar to a level comparable to the best education systems in the world";
- "to assist students in obtaining an improved use of learning data by utilizing higher quality curriculum materials";
- "to raise the level of teacher preparation programs to ensure that new teachers are able to implement the Common Core."[4]

As noted earlier, the idea for the creation of the Common Core was not a project of the federal government. Still, the Obama administration has strongly supported the effort. In the Race to the Top competition for federal funds and in the requirements for obtaining a waiver from No Child Left Behind, there were obvious advantages for states adopting the Common Core. Secretary Duncan has been vocal in his support of the movement. In a speech given in June 2013, he stated, "I'd like to make the case that these standards have the capacity to change education in the best of ways—setting loose the creativity and innovation of educators at the local level, raising the bar for students, strengthening our economy, and building a clearer path to the middle class."[5]

Currently, the federal government is providing funds to assist the development of assessment tools to measure student mastery of the objectives. The forty-five states and the District of Columbia that have agreed to use the Common Core in language arts will have the opportunity to utilize these national assessments. The challenge to those who are creating these computer-based assessments will be to fairly measure the accomplishment of the goals of the new curricula. Most observers agree that these goals are calling for student development of skills that go far beyond what is being taught in many classrooms today.

Supporters of this new approach argue that past assessments have relied heavily on objective tests based on multiple-choice questions. Even when students were asked to write essays, their answers were expected to include content knowledge that they had memorized for the test. The authors of the Common Core believe that teachers must "engage students in challenging applications of key content knowledge." To do this, "students must actively engage in their own learning." For this to occur, teachers must provide their students "interesting problems, investigations, debates, simulation, and games." Other approaches could include "Socratic questioning, presentations, projects, and other forms of learning that demand engagement."[6]

There is no doubt that these methods are remarkably similar to those called for by progressive educators over a century ago. Today's supporters of the Common Core further argue that the role of the standards is to "lay out a road map of major ideas, concepts, knowledge, and skills." It then becomes the job of the school and its teachers to redesign curriculum in ways that involve children "in cognitively challenging tasks." In the language arts curriculum, this means that teachers must find ways to ensure that students can do the following:

- "Analyze how and why individuals, events, and ideas develop and interact over the course of a text."
- "Integrate and evaluate content presented in diverse formats and media, including visually and quantitatively, as well as in words."
- "Read and comprehend complex literary and informational texts independently and proficiently."
- "Develop and strengthen writing as needed by planning, revising, editing, rewriting, or trying a new approach."
- "Use technology, including the Internet, to produce and publish writing and to interact and collaborate with others."
- "Conduct short as well as more sustained research projects based on focused questions, demonstrating understanding of the subject under investigation."[7]

Without a doubt, these objectives provide all teachers with significant new challenges. Because of the magnitude of the changes, especially in language arts, schools are attempting to ensure that faculty members of every subject have roles in meeting the language arts and math standards. Social studies, science, and even those teaching physical education, music, and art are being asked to include learning activities in language arts in their classes.

The pressures on teachers to move forward in their use of the Common Core have been increased by the fact that new assessments are being introduced. In several states, such as New York, the new tests were given in 2013, and other states are expected to utilize such tests in 2014. As might be expected, the results of the new tests based on the Common Core curriculum are likely to be less than impressive given the fact that students have been exposed to the new curriculum for only one year. In New York, state officials have attempted to warn the public that test scores in language arts and math will be considerably lower than in the past.

Even though the initial plan is for states to develop their own tests, it is likely that most will seriously consider the national tests being developed. It is possible that if No Child Left Behind is not reauthorized, the federal Department of Education might make adoption of the national tests a way to help states gain a renewal of the waivers given from the provisions of No Child Left Behind.

While there initially appeared to be strong support for the idea of the Common Core curriculum, a number of critics have begun to challenge the plan. Valerie Strauss, writing in the *Washington Post*, listed her concerns:

- States were not given sufficient time to consider the potential advantages and disadvantages of adopting the Common Core. They were pressured into a decision because of their desire to win a Race to the Top grant or to receive a waiver from No Child Left Behind.
- Classroom teachers and school administrators were in the minority among those who created the standards.
- There is not a great deal of research to prove that the new curriculum objectives will improve learning.
- Because the standards will be more challenging, low test results will further erode public confidence in their schools.
- Noted educational scholar Charlotte Danielson has examined the test questions that have thus far been prepared and has predicted that they are so difficult that the failure rate will be as high as 80 percent.[8]

In summary of her criticism, Strauss shares her belief that what she calls a "corporate reform project . . . will become another stage in the demise of public education."[9]

Others are worried about the added pressures that the new curriculums and assessments are placing on teachers and administrators as well as students. In New York State in 2013, when the new tests were introduced, some parents chose to keep their children home rather than allow them to take the new examinations. Others point to the wave of cheating that has appeared in a number of districts, perhaps as a by-product of the added importance given to test results.

Perhaps the primary opposition to the Common Core is coming from conservative individuals such as Rand Paul, who is considered a possible presidential candidate for 2016. He has labeled the Common Core as "a dangerous new curriculum that will only make public education worse and waste more of our money." He goes on to describe the initiative as "the same old radical Progressive ideology in a new package." [10]

An added concern at the state and local levels is the cost of implementing the curriculum changes. State governments have a responsibility of preparing teachers and administrators to carry out the transition to the new goals. Along with training costs, there is the need to purchase new learning materials. Since the standards include objectives dependent upon technology, some districts will need to upgrade their facilities and equipment. It was partly the financial issue that caused Michigan governor Rick Snyder to postpone the implementation of the Common Core Standards in 2013. [11] Further opposition was indicated in an article published in *Education News* that highlighted a member of the House of Representatives from New Jersey who presented a law that would allow states to "opt out" of the Common Core. [12]

If some politicians are having second thoughts, many teachers are experiencing significant stress, in part because of the fact that at the same time when they are revising their curriculum, their way of being evaluated is changing dramatically. Teachers and administrators are both facing the simultaneous demands created by these two reforms. (A later chapter discusses the impact of the new teacher evaluation programs, in part a result of the mandates required for states to receive waivers.) In some states, the result of these new demands on teachers and administrators is causing veteran faculty members and principals to retire early. This trend has been further stimulated by the fact that states and individual districts have implemented early retirement options to save salary costs in their budgets.

If there is a large number of retirements, it might provide an opportunity for schools to hire newly trained teachers who will, ideally, be more knowledgeable and comfortable with the Common Core. The challenge created by such a scenario is that teacher-training institutions are being expected to change their ways of preparing classroom teachers. A highly publicized study released in the summer of 2013 labeled teacher-training programs as an "industry of mediocrity." [13]

Conducted by the National Council of Teacher Quality, the report was highlighted in *U.S. News and World Report* and the *Wall Street Journal* and was the subject of a special presented on public radio. The study concluded that teacher-training programs varied greatly in quality but all needed to be improved. Among the criteria used to judge these programs was how well they prepared students to utilize the Common Core.[14]

The study attempted to measure what is happening in 1,130 institutions that graduate 170,000 new teachers every year. The president of the group issuing the report, Kate Walch, was quoted as saying that our new teacher graduates "don't know how to teach reading, don't know how to master a classroom, [and] don't know how to use data." In her view, at least, the results were dismal.[15] Needless to say, there was a quick response by representatives of teacher education programs to the methodology used in the study. Whether or not the results are valid, the project has helped to place increased public attention on our college teacher education programs.

An additional impact of the Common Core could be that the college entrance exam known as the SAT might well be revised to measure student competence in the Common Core objectives. The new president of the College Board, David Coleman, was "one of the chief architects of the Common Core." He has written, "The Common Core provides substantial opportunity to make the SAT even more reflective of what education wants." For him, "the real value here is that if the SAT aligns more to the Common Core, we won't be giving an assessment at the end of K–12 that's out of kilter with what we demand at the end of the day."[16] It is also likely that the other college entrance examination, the ACT, will revise its assessment to reflect the Common Core, as will even the GED test, given to students who have not completed high school but seek a diploma.

As one considers the impact of the changes noted in this chapter on how teachers teach, it is impossible to predict what will happen in our nation's classrooms. The goal of going beyond content mastery by using creative teaching techniques can certainly improve teaching. In both language arts and math, the objectives, if they can be met, could give added content depth and skills to what students are now receiving. If this is to happen, the tests must be created differently and must seek to measure how well students have mastered the goals included in the Common Core. Many think that there is sufficient flexibility for teachers to be creative in their planning.

For skeptics, the current initiatives are placing more importance than ever on examinations. Coupled with the fact that these tests will be used in evaluating teachers and school administrators, it is hard not to conclude that there will be even more "teaching to the test" in the future. This could include forcing the use of valued instructional time to teach test-taking skills.

With classrooms that include gifted as well as special education students, teachers will be faced with the additional challenge of differentiating instruction in meeting the Common Core goals. With the development of Common Core curriculums in science and social studies, there will likely be additional tests for which teacher preparation will be necessary. If one of the results of this movement could be longer school days or years, teachers would at least be given more time to meet the challenging standards. While this is happening in some areas, it is not likely to occur rapidly, because of the additional costs. With or without more time to teach, the results of the Common Core curriculum will depend on several factors.

First and foremost will be the ability of states and individual school districts to prepare their current teachers to effectively and creatively implement the new program. There are some positive signs in that numerous websites have emerged in which teachers are sharing creative ways to meet the Common Core objectives. Perhaps the most important factors in the implementation are the assessment methodologies used in the tests that are developed. Teachers will undoubtedly be feeling the need to concentrate on preparing their students to do well on these assessments. While some nations, such as China, are moving away from an overemphasis on testing, the United States appears to be increasing its focus.

One of the factors that will determine the success of the Common Core will be the way that teachers choose to meet its objectives. Teacher lesson planning has a history of its own, and it is a crucial topic in an understanding of the challenges that face American education.

NOTES

1. Julia Lawrence, "Duncan Delivers Fiery Speech Defending Common Core," *Education Week*, June 27, 2013, http://www.educationnews.org/education-policy-and-politics/duncan-delivers-fiery-speech-defending-common-core.html.

2. David T. Conley, "Building on the Common Core," *Educational Leadership* 68, no. 6 (2013): 16–20.

3. Conley, "Building on the Common Core."

4. Conley, "Building on the Common Core."

5. Lawrence, "Duncan Delivers Fiery Speech."

6. Conley, "Building on the Common Core."

7. Conley, "Building on the Common Core."

8. Valerie Strauss, "The Common Core's Fundamental Trouble," *Washington Post*, June 18, 2013, http://www.washingtonpost.com/blogs/answer-sheet/wp/2013/06/18/the-common-cores-fundamental-trouble.html.

9. Strauss, "The Common Core's Fundamental Trouble."

10. Jordan E. Wassell, "Michigan Rolls Back Common Core, Pulls Funding for Implementation," *Education News*, June 19, 2013, http://www.educationnews.org/education-policy-and-politics/michigan-rolls-back-on-common-core-pulls-funding-for-implementation.html.

11. Wassell, "Michigan Rolls Back Common Core."

12. Julia Lawrence, "Lawmaker Crafting Bill to Allow States to Opt Out of Common Core," *Education News*, June 13, 2013, http://www.educationnews.org/education-policy-and-politics/lawmaker-crafting-bill-to-allow-states-to-opt-out-of-common-core.html.

13. Catherine Gewertz, "New Report Blasts Teacher-Prep Programs," *Education Week*, June 18, 2013, http://blogs.edweek.org/edweek/curriculum/2013/06/teacher_prep_programs_are_an.html.

14. Gewertz, "New Report Blasts Teacher-Prep Programs."

15. Stephanie Simon, "Rookie Teachers Woefully Unprepared, Report Says," *MSN News*, June 18, 2013, http://news.msn.com/us/rookie-teachers-woefully-unprepared-report-says?ocid=ansnews11.

16. Catherine Gewertz, "SAT Future: Alignment to Standards," *Education Week* 31, no. 32 (2013): 1, 18.

ELEVEN

Lesson-Planning Models

Prior to this section, we have discussed in significant detail the many elements that, taken together, have markedly changed the teaching profession. Until this point, we have discussed a profession in flux, and it must be understood that this is still true. Although the section that we begin here deals with teaching as it is today, it by no means deals with teaching as it always will be or even teaching as it necessarily "should" be. Rather, it deals with the outcomes of the movements previously discussed.

From an outsider's perspective, lesson planning appears to be the main focus for a teacher at any level. It is the essence of what teaching really is: finding ways to best help students learn and meet certain educational objectives. For the beginning of the twentieth century, lesson planning was indeed regarded as the most important component of a teacher's job description. From that era came such theorists as Madeline Hunter and Charlotte Danielson, women who developed and shared theories about how best to organize an effective lesson.

In more recent years, however, as teachers have taken on new responsibilities, the creative lesson planning revered by many high-quality teachers has been replaced by prewritten plans designed to streamline and homogenize teaching. We discuss all these changes in the landscape of lesson planning as we face what is perhaps the most tangible element of the debate between teaching as an art and teaching as a science.

Before broaching the subject of particular lesson-planning strategies, we must briefly discuss the foundations of any lesson plan: curriculum. A future chapter addresses the issues currently affecting school curricula, so we treat the subject only briefly here. Any lesson plan must be designed to meet the curriculum objectives set in place by states. For most of our history, each state has been responsible for outlining standards for what every child should know and be able to do by the end of a certain grade level. Within districts and sometimes even buildings, there are often more specific expectations for which topics will be addressed at certain points in the school year. For a time, so long as lessons were reasonably able to meet those curriculum objectives, teachers were given full license to design lesson plans of any sort.

Good teaching practice, according to Donna Walker Tileston—author of *What Every Teacher Should Know about Instructional Planning* and a teacher of twenty-seven years—is "well planned and is aligned in several ways." She presents a triangular image of that alignment:

> First, the written curriculum, the teaching strategies, and the methods of evaluation are all aligned to each other; that is, we align what we say we are going to teach (i.e., state standards, local standards, curriculum, and classroom objectives) with what we actually teach our students and what we assess them on. This alignment can be shown visually as an equilateral triangle, with all sides being equal in importance and with the student in the middle. [1]

She goes on to describe a series of "microalignments" helping all students know and understand the information. These microalignments, she indicates, are the focus of lesson planning. [2]

There is a plethora of methods for microalignment, and some of the beauty of teaching is that no two teachers microalign in exactly the same ways. Two women in particular, however, presented methods that were accepted by many teachers as effective ways to help students learn. Madeline Hunter and Charlotte Danielson have each introduced lesson-planning strategies deemed effective enough by the greater teaching community that they are now widely taught in teacher education programs.

Madeline Hunter's *Mastery Teaching* is widely regarded as one of the best treatises on lesson planning and has been used as a textbook in many teacher preparation programs. In it, she describes the components of an effective lesson plan, later expanding on the factors involved in successful implementation of each component:

Objectives: the concrete goals of what students should be able to do by the end of the lesson.

Anticipatory set: a few sentences that will be used to draw the interest of students and prepare them for the lesson.

Input and modeling: the actions that will be used to communicate information to students.

Checking understanding and guided practice: the process through which the teacher informally or formally assesses how well students are grasping the content and helps them practice the skill objectives on their own.

Independent practice: students are given the opportunity to practice the new skill or knowledge on their own.[3]

Hunter describes each component of the lesson plan as a particular decision that must be made by the instructor. She elaborates, "Teaching can be defined as a constant stream of professional decisions made before, during, and after interaction with the student; decisions that, when implemented, increase the probability of learning."[4] These decisions fall under two major categories: what teachers will teach and how students will learn it.

What will be taught, as previously explained, is primarily decided by curriculum standards. How to teach, however, is a decision made by each teacher. Hunter asserts that two factors affect student learning: input modalities and output modalities. Input—the way that students receive information—is, according to Hunter, "the only way in which teaching models differ."[5] She advocates for a lesson-planning model in which input modalities are chosen with the objective in mind:

> If we want students to develop social interaction skills, we'll probably want them working together rather than listening to a lecture. If the ability to identify similarities and differences is paramount, then an activity requiring them to do so is warranted. If the initial acquisition of a new formula is the focus, a skilled teacher presentation may be most effective. If we want students to develop social skills as well as to interact with the content, we will probably want them working in cooperative groups.[6]

Here, we see what Hunter regards as one of the most essential parts of teaching. On some level, the teacher must be able to look at an objective and make a decision about the best method for helping students achieve it. Another component of the decision-making process cannot be ignored, and that is the learning styles of students. Recognizing that how students best process information is affected by their preferred learning styles, Hunter notes that modality preference is a result of practice. She asserts, "The most effective instruction is that which addresses multiple modalities: instruction where students get to hear, see, touch, and discuss."[7]

A teacher delivering multiple lessons every day must engage in this deeply involved and thoughtful process on a daily basis, also working hard to adjust lessons as they are delivered. Such an undertaking requires creativity, a deep understanding of educational psychology, and knowledge of classroom dynamic. Today, however, many teachers are being asked to abandon this process in favor of canned lessons. It's been a long time coming. For years, textbooks and teachers' manuals have provided possible lesson plans and teaching ideas that teachers are free to use, draw inspiration from, or simply ignore in favor of handcrafted planning. That choice, however, was taken away for many teachers when No Child Left Behind entered the picture in 2001.

Part of No Child Left Behind legislation is a program called Reading First, which allocates $6 billion over the course of six years to states that guarantee implementation of programs using what it calls "proven methods and programs." In an article for PBS.org, Sarah Colt outlines the experiences of teachers in several districts who were asked to trade in their plan books for these "proven methods," some after more than twenty years of documented successful teaching.[8]

The idea behind scripted lessons has been to put all teachers within a given district on the same page with curriculum so that they know exactly what is expected. Colt quotes one proponent of scripted strategies, Eric Smith, superintendent of Charlotte-Mecklenburg schools in North Carolina, who explains that "because of the diversity of experience among teachers, especially in inner city schools, it is 'the job of central administration . . . the job of the superintendent of schools to bring that kind of clarity to the classroom and give the teachers the strategies that will help them to be successful.'"[9]

One of the programs used by many districts is Success for All, which was developed in the mid-1980s by Johns Hopkins University educator Bob Slavin for failing Baltimore schools. The program requires a dedicated ninety minutes of reading instruction every day, during which teachers "follow a pre-ordained lesson plan that has every minute of time filled with strategies to teach reading to every child in the class." Explaining his program, Slavin stated, "One of the things that's most characteristic of Success for All is that we try not to leave very much to chance. . . . We want every minute of the school day used for productive activities that we know from research to be the most effective things we can provide."[10]

Slavin invoked the recently popular business metaphor in vouching for his program. "If you're in business, you watch your quarterly results very closely to know whether your business strategies are paying off. . . . In any successful field, people watch outcomes very, very closely. In education we have to do the same."[11]

The teachers who have been asked to implement the program, however, seem to feel differently. "A trained monkey could do this program," explains one teacher, who found the process of adopting the program "humiliating and demeaning." Many critics have expressed concerns that the curriculums are too narrowly focused on the basics, turning teachers from creative professionals into robots. Another teacher noted, "It was impossible to get everything done the way it was supposed to be. You have kids looking at you like 'what did you say?' and you're thinking, 'sorry, it's 8:10 gotta move on honey.'"[12]

This very practical concern comes along with concerns that many have voiced about creativity being wrested from the hands of teachers. Scripted programs are often described as "teacher proof" because they do not require experience or training to follow the prepared materials. This does not concern Slavin, who rebuts,

> In education, for some reason, we've resisted the idea that good practice can be replicated, and we're always getting all misty eyed and romantic about some outstanding principal in the inner city who's doing something that may be absolutely wonderful. But you can climb to the top of their building and probably see three other buildings from there that are doing the most horrible things to children. And they will never change what they're doing on the basis of what that one wonderful principal is doing until you take what that wonderful principal is doing and make into something that's got legs that can travel and that can be replicated in other locations.

Despite concerns about the dehumanization of teaching, there has been little argument about the effectiveness of the program. One district found that reading scores rose by 25% after implementation of the program, even at the same time that the district saw increases in students of poverty and in students learning English as a second language. A study showed that in thirty-eight schools using Success for All, students read better after two years in the program and were outpacing students in regular classrooms by up to half a school year.[13]

In terms of anecdotal evidence, one teacher admitted that she saw a change in her students several months into implementing a scripted curriculum. "'When some of those [struggling] kids start believing that they too can read and that they want to read—that's what teaching is about, I think. It's helping empower kids so that they can go on to learn and to feel that they can learn anything.' She also noticed a change in her teaching—she started internalizing the strategies and using them in all her classes, not just during the reading period."[14]

Another teacher likened the program to "the Starbucks of education" because of the standardization, which, he claims, is what makes scripted lessons successful. It means that experienced teachers and first-year teachers alike have a proven reliable method for teaching—one that many beginning teachers in particular find useful. Yet, some teachers who have years of experience feel comfortable allowing for a little personality and creativity within the program. Another benefit that has been cited deals with increased levels of mobility. As poor families move around because of unstable employment and housing, their children have an easier time transitioning among classrooms that are implementing the same lesson plans and curriculum.[15]

Having discussed the artistic and scientific methods of planning, we find it worth returning to a part of Madeline Hunter's definition of lesson planning, which she described as a series of decisions made to increase the probability of learning: this seems to be the crux of the issue. Hunter acknowledges that by use of the term *probability*, learning success is up to the individual student. A teacher can try to provide the best possible conditions for students to learn, but in the end, it is down to the student to decide whether or not he or she will learn.

The approach taken by proponents of scripted lessons is one that appears to rely on more predictable outcomes in an "if x, then y" model. If teachers all use the same scientifically proven methods, then all students will learn. In this way of thinking, success is not a matter of probability. It is a certainty under the right conditions.

What has been created in the debate about creative versus scripted lesson plans is essentially the debate about teaching as an art versus teaching as a science in a more definable arena. Those on the artistic side of the stage might point out that scripted lessons are successful only in achieving scientific goals. They may pose the question, "Does success on a standardized test really indicate that learning has happened?" On the contrary, those on the scientific side might express the view that it is impossible to know how our students are performing and learning unless we give them all an identical experience.

Charlotte Danielson, a famed educational scholar who has mainly focused her research on lesson planning and teacher evaluation, seems to fall somewhere in the middle. In the foreword for *Powerful Lesson Planning: Every Teacher's Guide to Effective Instruction,* she explains,

> Textbooks and other instructional materials provide teachers with learning objectives, activities, assessments, and of course, materials needed—all they need for instructional planning. Teachers have the option, if they so choose, to simply follow the directions and "connect the dots." In many cases, the instructional suggestions offered by the textbooks and ancillary materials are as viable as those that many teachers (particularly novices) could create on their own. However, only teachers know their own students (and therefore how to differentiate instruction to assist them), and content standards are different in different locations. Therefore, if teachers can acquire sophisticated planning skills, they will be able to offer a richer instructional environment for their students than if they relied solely on their text materials.[16]

Danielson's focus on the role of the teacher in effective lesson planning and delivery is one that seems to be missing from scripted lessons and, indeed, from the educational debate as a whole. Although teachers were encouraged to use creativity and their own knowledge of educational psychology and child development only a few short years ago, the direction in which we seem to be headed is veering further and further from that model. Led by the scripted lesson movement, there is an impending departure from what is deemed the "uncertainty" of teacher-created lessons.

These issues will only be complicated by a new emphasis on how teachers are being evaluated. Brought on by the requirements of Race to the Top and the waiver requirements, states and their school districts have been busy creating new and more complex ways to evaluate teachers. We consider this important trend in our next chapter.

NOTES

1. Donna Walker Tileston, *What Every Teacher Should Know about Instructional Planning* (Thousand Oaks, CA: Corwin Press, 2004), 1.

2. Tileston, *What Every Teacher Should Know.*

3. Robin Hunter, reviser and updater, *Madeline Hunter's Mastery Teaching: Increasing Instructional Effectiveness in Elementary and Secondary Schools,* updated ed. (Thousand Oaks, CA: Corwin Press, 2004), 1–2.

4. Hunter, *Madeline Hunter's Mastery Teaching,* 3.

5. Hunter, *Madeline Hunter's Mastery Teaching,* 6.

6. Hunter, *Madeline Hunter's Mastery Teaching,* 7.

7. Hunter, *Madeline Hunter's Mastery Teaching,* 7.

8. Sarah Colt, "Do Scripted Lessons Work—or Not?" http://www.pbs.org/makingschoolswork/sbs/sfa/lessons.html.

9. Colt, "Do Scripted Lessons Work—or Not?"

10. Colt, "Do Scripted Lessons Work—or Not?"

11. Colt, "Do Scripted Lessons Work—or Not?"

12. Colt, "Do Scripted Lessons Work—or Not?"

13. Colt, "Do Scripted Lessons Work—or Not?"

14. Colt, "Do Scripted Lessons Work—or Not?"

15. Colt, "Do Scripted Lessons Work—or Not?"

16. Charlotte Danielson, in Janice Skowron, *Powerful Lesson Planning: Every Teacher's Guide to Effective Instruction,* 2nd ed. (Thousand Oaks, CA: Corwin Press, 2006), ix.

TWELVE

The New Emphasis on Teacher Evaluation

Until the beginning of the twenty-first century, the supervision of teachers by school administrators was quite subjective. Administrators, if they had any training concerning supervision duties, accepted that they would be doing lesson observations, which would allow them to give suggestions on how teachers might improve what they were doing. At the same time, they were, hopefully, complimenting teachers on their strengths. In addition, and often more important, was that the classroom observations were the primary method for judging probationary teachers in public schools. These class visitations were instrumental in the decision of whether or not a teacher would receive tenure. In most states, the probationary period consisted of the first three years of a teacher's employment in the district.

During this trial period, a new teacher might be observed by an administrator three times each year. There were, of course, other factors taken into account in evaluating teachers. A competent administrator sought to judge how well the teacher interacted with colleagues and parents. Also considered was the teacher's involvement in grade level or departmental activities. In some states, there were mandatory student examinations. For example, in New York State, Regents exams were given in most high school academic subjects, and the success of students on these tests was another way of judging a teacher's competence. Finally, and often the critical factor, was the administrator's evaluation of the teacher's classroom management skills. A teacher who sent too many students to the principal for discipline might well jeopardize his or her future in the district.

Once a faculty member was recommended by the superintendent and received a majority tenure vote by the Board of Education, the amount of supervision given to that teacher was greatly reduced. In many districts, a tenured teacher was observed once a year or perhaps not at all. This lack of supervision and evaluation was not a result of the administrators not being interested in this part of the job but rather the fact that principals had many other responsibilities. For many principals, student discipline and parent work took a majority of their time. As a result, many schools lacked the personnel needed to carry out more extensive supervision and evaluation programs.

Beginning with the *Nation at Risk* report and then with the passage of No Child Left Behind, there was a growing consensus that to improve schools, perhaps the most important issue was to increase the effectiveness of classroom teachers. Within the education community, most people agreed that, beginning with the college selection process of future teachers, we should be seeking to raise the academic level of those entering the profession and then to improve the teacher education programs that were preparing them to enter the classroom. It was also obvious that there should be an ongoing program to help all teachers grow professionally. More recently, there have been many who have argued that teachers must be held accountable for student success.

It is difficult to disagree with the idea that we must seek to recruit and maintain excellent teachers in the profession. The question becomes, "What is the best way to ensure quality teaching?" In the United States in the twenty-first century, one of the accepted answers to this question is that teachers must be subject to an ongoing program of evaluation that will help to identify poor teachers and either quickly assist them to improve or move them out of the schools. At the same time, for those who are judged to be competent, most observers believe that continual professional development is required. The model is one that some would argue is currently successful in the world of business.

Many politicians and Board of Education members go further in arguing that a way to improve classroom teaching is to introduce the concept of "pay for performance." In a system where compensation has primarily been based on seniority, many think that we should be paying teachers based on the quality of their work in the classrooms. At the same time, there is in some states a campaign to end or at least modify the practice of giving tenure to teachers. This occurred in North Carolina: "Teachers in that state will no longer qualify for lifetime tenure after five years on the job. This system has been replaced by giving to teachers four-year contracts." [1]

If, as a nation, we are to develop a more sophisticated teacher evaluation procedure, especially if compensation depends on it, it follows that such a plan must be more objective than how we supervised teachers in the past. For many who have considered this challenge, the answer is to somehow judge if the teacher's students are truly learning the prescribed curriculum. These advocates make the argument that just as a salesperson might be evaluated and paid on the basis of his or her sales during a year, a teacher should be judged on what his or her students have learned. If this is to be a factor in teacher evaluation, then student test results might well be the most objective way to judge student learning and thus determine how well a teacher is doing his or her job.

This conclusion was accepted by the federal Department of Education when, as part of its stimulus legislation, it introduced a system of educational grants entitled Race to the Top. This program offered states badly needed federal subsidies in the form of competitive federal grants. To obtain the grants, states were given a number of conditions that had to be met. The department made it clear that states should have teacher evaluation systems that included the criteria of student test results. Additional pressure for considering testing as a part of a comprehensive evaluation program was included in the mandates for those states that were seeking a waiver from No Child Left Behind in 2011. Among the requirements for obtaining a waiver, it was mandated that "the state must have an effective system for 'evaluating and supporting teacher and principal effectiveness.' The requirements also made clear that such systems must consider test scores."[2] As most states applied for waivers, there have been extensive negotiations at the state level between districts and teachers unions to devise new plans to improve teacher evaluation.

The waivers granted to the states were to last only two years. By August 2013, nineteen states that had received waivers had teacher evaluation plans accepted by the federal education department. Many states are still working on plans for which they must seek approval.[3] Because the process for gaining approval of the plans has been so time-consuming, the department decided that waivers received by the summer of 2012 would be allowed to extend the deadline for states putting into place their new evaluation systems. Under the original conditions, these plans were to be used no later than the 2015–2016 school year. The deadline has been extended for one year.[4]

With thirty-nine states having been granted a waiver, it can be expected that, as long as teachers unions are involved in teacher evaluation, this will continue to be a controversial issue in most states and school districts. In Denver, Colorado, the administrators and teachers are being trained in peer evaluations. Among the factors being considered are how well teachers utilize technology in their lessons and how the instructor responds to pupils who are having difficulty. Student feedback is also considered, and "the teacher and administrative ratings will be 50 percent based on student test scores."[5] It is the reliance on test scores that has become the most controversial issue in most states and districts.

An added source of conflict has arisen as a result of the districts that have attempted to make the results of their teacher evaluations public knowledge. As early as 2010, the *Los Angeles Times* "matched Los Angeles students' test scores to their teachers and published value-added scores using a system developed by a respected economist making use of a complex statistical model." In 2011, the *Times* updated its ratings, publishing the most recent test data. As a result of these publications, it became possible for parents to pressure principals to move their students from low-ranking teachers to higher-ranking teachers. A similar situation occurred in New York City. The result was front-page stories in several tabloids naming the "worst teachers in New York City." The difference was that in New York, the union sued to block future releases.[6]

In Boston, the school district chose to deny requests for publication of teacher ratings based on the freedom-of-information request. It argued that this information was a part of a teacher's personnel file and therefore could not be considered under the freedom-of-information laws. It also refused to release the "school by school ratings," arguing that it would inhibit the district's "ability to function effectively as an employer." The *Boston Globe*, which had made the request, responded by appealing the decision.[7]

Even when the question of making evaluations public is not considered, teachers unions are challenging evaluation systems in court. In Florida, the evaluation of all teachers is being affected by tests given in grades 4–8 for math and grades 4–10 in reading. Teachers of subjects other than math and reading are being affected by the scores on these tests, even though it is not their primary duty to teach these skills. For example, a music teacher's evaluation could be negatively affected by the reading and math scores in one's school. Many other districts and states have adopted systems that have this type of evaluation. It will be up to the courts to decide the appropriateness of this approach.[8]

In every state, test scores are a part of the new evaluation process. The importance given to this factor can range between 20 and 50 percent of a teacher's evaluation. In recent years, these plans have attempted to incorporate a concept known as *value added*, which allows a teacher to be judged on a student's improvement on test scores over a specific period. Although seemingly fairer than the AYP standard in the No Child Left Behind law, unions continue to point out discrepancies and problems in using tests as part of the evaluations.

As we move toward new national assessments based on the Common Core, there is an added concern over the cost of the tests. One of the agencies developing Common Core examinations has announced that its price for a summative math and reading test would be $29.50 per student. Currently, many states are spending much less for the tests that they are giving. For example, Georgia spends $12 per student for the state-level tests.[9]

Still, another factor that is being considered in teacher evaluations is the use of student surveys. An article in *Kappan Magazine* in 2012 argued, "Well-crafted student surveys can play an important role in suggesting directions for professional development and also in evaluating teacher effectiveness." According to the author, "students know good instruction when they experience it as well as when they do not." This author, at least, predicts that there will be "a growing consensus that student perception surveys should be among the multiple measures used multiple times over multiple years, not only to measure teacher effectiveness, but also to inform a broader set of actions that we can take to improve schools."[10]

Whether it is student evaluations, test score results, peer reviews, or principals' observations, a great deal is currently being written about how to make teacher evaluations more effective. For example, Robert J. Marzano—CEO of the Marzano Research Library in Denver, Colorado, and author of the book *The Art and Science of Teaching*—lists the following among his priorities for an effective teacher evaluation program:

- The use of a teacher's self-evaluation, which can be compared with the observer's rating
- The use of both announced and unannounced lesson observations, as well as frequent walks through the teacher's classroom
- The use of lesson videos, which can be reviewed by one or multiple observers
- Allowing teachers to challenge their evaluations[11]

An article in *Educational Leadership* quotes individual teachers' views on the process. Among those practices encouraged was peer assistance. Most educators agree that assigning experienced mentors to new teachers is very helpful. This experienced teacher would not be part of the evaluation process but rather would be there to assist teachers in their initial years working in the district. Another suggestion from a practicing teacher is the understanding that every element in an evaluation rubric may not fit a particular lesson. A third teacher makes the point in *Educational Leadership* that "the best teachers are attracted by a school culture in which teacher evaluation is done with them, not to them."[12]

Additional suggestions are included in another article in *Educational Leadership*. Here, the importance of collaboration between districts and unions in developing a system is emphasized. The integration of the evaluation process, along with the need for continual professional growth, should be part of the school culture. These authors also emphasize the importance of flexibility in any system.[13]

For Charlotte Danielson, certainly one of the most respected educators specializing in the field of teacher evaluation, it is essential that if a district seeks a plan "that teachers find meaningful and from which they can learn, we must use processes that are not only rigorous, valid, and reliable, but also engage teachers in those activities that promote learning—namely self-assessment, reflection on practice, and professional conversation."[14]

As the discussions concerning how to best evaluate teachers continue, there is no question that teachers must be a part of the ongoing dialogue. This means that their voices will most likely be heard through their unions. Randi Weingarten, president of the American Federation of Teachers, has expressed the fear of many in the profession: "Too often, teachers are left 'to sink or swim' without help from more senior teachers or their schools' leaders." For her, it is important that the focus be on trying to improve teachers. Her plea is that districts should not "fixate on how to dismiss teachers" but rather "on how we nurture, support, and keep them." [15]

Others who are considering this issue have pointed to the possibility of studying the systems used in nations that have established a reputation for having excellent schools. A survey of those countries would undoubtedly show that they use evaluation as a tool for both accountability and instructional improvement. Although many nations do use standardized test results as part of the process, the way that it is done varies greatly. Perhaps the most original approach to ensuring accountability and growth can be found in Finland, which has been recognized for its fine schools for a number of years. It is interesting to note that "high-stakes testing plays no role in teacher evaluation" in Finland. The only standardized tests are assessments given at grades 6–9 to "inform policy and curriculum decisions." An additional "matriculation examination" is given for university admission. [16]

It appears that in Finland, at least, the success of the schools is primarily based on the fact that it has been able to make "teaching a prestigious and competitive field to enter." It also provides "ongoing learning opportunities for teachers to develop their professional skills" and a "collegial, safe learning environment that encourages trial, allows and corrects errors, gives teachers professional time, space, and autonomy, and provides social and monetary respect for their profession." [17]

Along with Finland, we can look to Canada, South Korea, Japan, and a number of other countries to find ways to develop the best possible systems for evaluating our teachers. There is no question that, to be effective, the process must be a cooperative one. Still, there are those like the writer of an editorial in the *New York Times* who expressed "outrage that educators in the past believed both that teaching is an 'art' that cannot be rigorously evaluated and that teachers should not be held accountable for student progress." There are many fewer people today who take the position that teachers should not be accountable for student success. Yet, most educators at least believe that we must be cautious in our attempts to develop systems that are fair and effective and that will, in the words of Marge Scherer, "further the art of teaching." [18]

Along with the attempts to improve teacher evaluation, another major trend that began at the end of the twentieth century is the issue of offering choice to families in the schools their children will attend—the subject of our next chapter.

NOTES

1. Julia Lawrence, "North Carolina Dumps Teacher Tenure, Pay for Graduate Degrees," *Education News,* August 1, 2013, http://www.educationnews.org/education-policy-and-politics/north-carolinas-new-budget-dumps-teacher-tenure/.

2. Margaret A. Jorgensen and Jenny Hoffmann, *History of the No Child Left Behind Act of 2001* (San Antonio, TX: Harcourt Assessment, 2003).

3. Michele McNeil, "More NCLB Waiver States Get Federal Approval for Teacher Evaluations," *Education Week,* July 29, 2013, http://blogs.edweek.org/edweek/campaign-k-12/2013/07/more_nclb_waiver_states_secure.html.

4. Alyson Klein, "Waiver States Split on Ed. Dept. Offer of New Flexibility," *Education Week* 32, no. 36 (July 10, 2013): 30.

5. Kristen Wyatt, "Colo. Begins Controversial Teacher-Grading System," *Denver Post,* August 1, 2013, http://www.denverpost.com/education/ci_23774958/colo-begins-controversial-teacher-grading-system.html.

6. Aaron Pallas, "Scarlet Letter," *Educational Leadership* 70, no. 3 (November 2012): 55–57.

7. Julia Lawrence, "Boston Denies Request to Make Teacher Assessments Public," *Education News,* July 15, 2013, http://www.educationnews.org/education-policy-and-politics/boston-denies-request-to-make-teacher-assessments-public.html.

8. Stephen Sawchuk, "Union Sues over Basis of Appraisal," *Education Week* 32, no. 29 (April 24, 2013): 1–15.

9. Valerie Strauss, "New Common Core Tests: Worth the Price?" *Washington Post,* July 24, 2013, http://www.washingtonpost.com/blogs/answer-sheet/wp/2013/07/24/new-common-core-tests-worth-the-price/.

10. Ronald F. Ferguson, "Can Student Surveys Measure Teaching Quality?" *Kappan* (November 2012): 24–28.

11. Robert J. Marzano, "Reducing Error in Teacher Observation Scores," *Educational Leadership* 70, no. 3 (November 2012): 82–83.

12. The collective wisdom of authors published in the November 2012 issue of *Educational Leadership:* "Teacher Evaluation: What's Fair, What's Effective?"

13. Mark Simon, "Effective Teacher Evaluation: Lessons from Experience," *Educational Leadership* 70, no. 3 (November 2012): 61.

14. Morgaen L. Donaldson, "Strengthening Teacher Evaluation: What District Leaders Can Do," *Educational Leadership* 69, no. 8 (May 2012): 78–82.

15. "Chief of Teachers' Union: Bad Educators Hurt Good Ones, Should Find New Professions," *Washington Post,* July 22, 2013, http://www.washingtonpost.com/politics/chief-of-teachers-union-bad-educators-hurt-good-ones-should-find-new-professions/2013/07/22/93ceda70-f311-11e2-8464-57e57af86290_story.html.

16. James H. Williams and Laura C. Engel, "How Do Other Countries Evaluate Teachers," *Kappan* 94, no. 4 (November 2012): 53–57.

17. Williams and Engel, "How Do Other Countries Evaluate Teachers."

18. "In Search of Excellent Teaching," *New York Times,* September 16, 2012, http://nytimes.com/2012/09/17/opinion/in-search-of-excellent-teaching.html, in Marge Scherer, "Teachers under the Looking Glass," *Educational Leadership* 70, no. 3 (November 2012): 7.

THIRTEEN

The Impact of Educational Choice on Teaching

Although the public school continued to gain popularity throughout the twentieth century, eventually coming to represent the most popular educational choice for American families, it would be unfair to shunt aside other school environments in a discussion of the teaching profession. Today, students attending private schools make up only 10 percent of the school-age population in the United States, and the number is declining.[1] Still, many families who have chosen private schools are confident that such schools provide a better education. The aim of this chapter is not to settle the private-versus-public school debate but rather to examine the pedagogical differences between the two. Especially in light of the present debates regarding school choice, a thorough examination of the wide variety of available options is timely and important.

Because private and parochial schools are not funded by the state, they, for the most part, operate outside state and federal education requirements. They can create their own curricula and choose which assessments to give, and they are allowed to hire whomever they choose. These factors create a teaching environment extremely different from that of a public school. To fully understand the differences in pedagogical styles between the two, it is essential to understand the differences in environment.

As discussed in the previous chapter, much of the pedagogical climate in today's public schools is dictated by state and federal regulation. As private entities, however, independent schools are largely unfettered by the requirements of the state and federal governments and local school boards. Rather, they are subject to the decisions of whichever organizations sponsor and govern them. Created for a variety of reasons, "including college-prep programs, religious instruction and family values," private schools take different forms depending on the expectations of the families that choose them. As noted by the authors of *Foundations of American Education*, it can be difficult to generalize about these reasons:

> These schools take different forms in response to parents who want their children to have broader educational opportunities, who seek a more rigorous or more restrictive environment for their children, or who desire a more permissive environment than the public schools can provide. This pattern of diverse aspirations has contributed to the development of private schools noted more for their differences than their similarities. They include traditional church-related schools, schools associated with evangelical groups, private traditional day schools, and "free" schools in which students can pursue individual interests. [2]

Although the goals of each nonpublic school are unique, certain characteristics exist in commonality between all private and parochial schools. They are self-supported and have self-selected faculty, self-defined curricula, self-selected students, and generally smaller class sizes. [3] Each factor creates in nonpublic schools a set of conditions forming vastly different teaching experiences for faculty members.

While public schools are supported by the federal, state, and local governments, private and parochial schools are tasked with supporting themselves. Even though many parochial schools are able to draw some financial support from their parishes, dioceses, or other religious organizations, the main source of support for the majority of private and parochial schools comes from tuition. According to a 2010 study, the average yearly tuition for a non-Catholic private education in the United States was $8,549, while the average yearly tuition for a Catholic education was $6,018. [4]

The changes affected by tuition-based funding go much deeper than the financial affairs of the organization. Because private schools come with a high cost, their clientele tend to be of a particular socioeconomic class. The students whose parents can afford to send them to private schools are generally affluent, resulting in a school population far less diverse than those of public schools. Some have argued that the government should distribute vouchers, essentially allowing parents who cannot afford to send their children to private schools a choice where their children are educated, but for now, the opportunity tends to be limited.

Proponents of private education have suggested that private schools offer an opportunity for greater diversity because they can draw from wider geographic regions. In the introduction to her book *Independent Schools, Independent Thinkers*, Pearl Rock Kane asserts,

> In many affluent communities such as Greenwich, Connecticut, or Newport Beach, California, where the average cost of houses is over half a million dollars, only families that can afford to purchase these expensive houses can send their children to the local public school. The

result is that the schools are white, upper-class institutions with little diversity. In affluent communities, private schools are often more diverse than the local public schools because private schools recruit from a wider geographic area.[5]

Though such an argument has its merits, it is difficult to argue that private schools are, across the board, more diverse. Because private education comes with significant financial cost, the students and their parents are necessarily of certain financial status, a factor that does affect the pedagogy of private institutions. As written by Luis Benveniste, Martin Carnoy, and Richard Rothstein, *All Else Equal, Are Public and Private Schools Different?* details the findings of the authors' study in which they extensively interviewed various administrators, teachers, parents, and students at eight public and eight private schools. According to their research, "higher-income parents tend to be more involved than lower-income parents in a variety of school activities. They are also more at ease in challenging schools with regard to educational practices."[6]

This focus on parent satisfaction is another major effect of tuition-based finance. Private schools depend on the satisfaction of their "customers" for funding and are held accountable directly by those paying for education. Also used in the argument for private school vouchers, this accountability requires teachers to create successful outcomes. Benveniste, Carnoy, and Rothstein explain that in high-income private schools,

> parents comprise a vocal group that make explicit their expectations for an education of the highest quality for their children. They exercise little reservation in expressing clearly their views, concerns, and demands to school administrators and teachers. They feel entitled to making judgments about the quality of education provision that their children receive and demand that deficiencies be redressed. They also show little hesitation in turning to the highest possible authorities to make their opinions known. They not only expect to be listened to, but they also expect that their exhortations will lead to concrete action toward the fulfillment of their wishes.

The self-supporting nature of private and parochial schools also directly affects the compensation of teachers. In 2010, the average base salary for teachers in public schools was $49,630, while the average for teachers in private schools was $36,250.[7] Some private and parochial schools even pay their teachers hourly, at rates as low as $8.25 per hour. It is not difficult to believe that teacher turnover rates in private schools tend to be significantly higher than those in public schools. One of the private schools discussed in *All Else Equal* experienced a 40 percent annual turnover rate among the school's eighteen full-time classroom teachers and six area specialists. Parents, teachers, and administrators who were asked about the factors contributing to such rapid turnover cited "low pay, lack of professional growth, depressing facilities, and noise level."[8]

At the school discussed, as well as in many other private schools, "a frequent pattern . . . is one in which young teachers gain their initial work experience teaching in the private sector and later apply for positions at public schools because of the pay differentials." Many teachers find jobs in public schools after a year or two of teaching in a private school. The implications of such patterns include a general lack of experienced teachers in private schools, not only because of high turnover, but because the teachers who consistently fill vacant positions have little or no previous teaching experience.

Besides the implications of self-support as a defining factor of private and parochial schools, other major differences are affected by the self-selection of faculty members in which private and parochial schools engage. Although it is true that public school administrators are responsible for hiring teachers, they are bound by state requirements for teacher certification. No such legal requirement exists for private institutions. Hearkening back to the colonial era, during which prestigious schoolteachers were masters in their fields rather than masters of educational theory, many secondary private schools prefer to hire teachers with undergraduate and graduate degrees in their subject areas instead of teachers trained through teacher education programs.

> Most independent school teachers have not taken the education courses necessary for certification to teach in public schools and may regard such courses as of lesser intellectual merit than courses in their academic fields. The schools, too, are not convinced that professional preparation in education is necessary. With the exception of training in early childhood education, many independent school administrators believe that pedagogy is a skill that can be learned on the job. Most schools supply only limited assistance in learning to teach, and young teachers learn the ropes informally from other teachers or by trial and error.[9]

In their interviews about the teacher selection process, the authors of *All Else Equal* found that public school principals were more likely to hire applicants with strong pedagogical skills and academic qualifications. Meanwhile, parochial school leaders listed family background, religious orientation, and a strong rapport with children as the primary qualifications for teachers. One principal stated that pedagogical philosophy was secondary "because the school had adopted an explicit curriculum guide and teachers needed only to follow it."[10]

Such widely different expectations for teachers are, in part, symptomatic of a third defining factor of nonpublic schools: self-selected curriculum. State-certified teachers are certified with the state-mandated curriculum in mind. Since private and parochial schools select their own curricula, it is only sensible that they should choose the teachers who they feel are best equipped to implement those curricula. Generally speaking, the curriculum chosen by a given school is selected because it aligns with that school's value orientation. Many parochial schools choose curricula that have a particularly moral flavor or deal in a particular way with the topic of evolution.[11]

In the past, the latitude given to private schools to define their own curricula has been virtually absolute, given that private schools are exempt from state tests. Schools have tended to gauge their success by the preparedness of their students for college.[12] However, with the advent of the Common Core curriculum, the SAT and the ACT (college preparedness examinations) have begun changes intended to more closely align them with the new standards. Even though nonpublic schools have prided themselves on the success of their curricula in preparing students for college, they may begin to find that the examinations assessing readiness are designed to test the curricula of the public schools.

One argument that is frequently made about the college preparation of private school students is based around another defining element of private schools. There is an application process involved during the enrollment process for private and parochial schools, allowing them to choose the students they teach. Proponents of private education are quick to point out that the selection is mutual. "The school chooses the student, but the student also chooses the school. . . . Mutual freedom of association by students and schools is fundamental to the sense of community that shapes the educational effectiveness of independent schools," says Kane.[13]

A direct result of private schools' abilities to select which students will be accepted is the characteristic small class size of private and parochial schools. While the average student-to-teacher ratio in public schools is 15.7:1, Catholic schools boast a smaller ratio of 14.7:1 and private schools an even lower 11.1:1. These lower numbers have benefits as well as drawbacks, creating a recent controversy over the importance of class size. Most research is on the side of smaller classes, including the results of the STAR project (Student/Teacher Achievement Ratio), conducted on grade K–3 classrooms in Tennessee in the late 1970s:

> The learning gains students made in classes of 13 to 17 students persisted long after the students moved back into average-size classes. What's more, the Tennessee researchers found, poor and African-American students appeared to reap the greatest learning gains in smaller classes. After kindergarten, the gains black students made in smaller classes were typically twice as large as those for whites. Follow-up studies through the years have found the students who had been in small classes in their early years had better academic and personal outcomes throughout their school years and beyond.[14]

Besides the results of the STAR project, the general consensus has been that smaller class sizes allow teachers to spend more time with struggling students, instead of allowing them to fall behind. Leonard Baird has also pointed out that students who are part of a smaller graduating class are at less risk for becoming "socially invisible nonpersons" like those who pass through public schools.[15]

Even though the small class sizes characteristic of private schools can be academically and socially beneficial, there is some pushback from those claiming that extremely small classes are not necessarily better. The smaller, generally homogeneous graduating classes of many nonpublic schools offer less exposure to socioeconomic, religious, and, in some cases, racial diversity than those of public schools. Because of their small sizes, many nonpublic schools are also less able to offer a wide range of extracurricular activities, sports teams, and elective courses.

Despite the fact that the five characteristics of nonpublic schools addressed here—self-funded, self-selected faculty, self-defined curricula, self-selected students, and generally smaller class size—are present in the majority of nonpublic schools, there are further breakdowns beyond the public-nonpublic dichotomy that account for major pedagogical differences. Within the category of "nonpublic schools," there are parochial schools, college preparatory schools, and charter schools (which, though public, differ significantly from traditional public schools), as well as homeschooling. Each of these is considered a viable educational option by proponents of school choice, and each has implications for the teachers whom it employs.

Recent years have seen major shifts in parochial school enrollment. Just a decade ago, 84 percent of private school students attended church affiliated schools, and 51 percent of those schools were Roman Catholic.[16] In the fall of 2009, however, of the 33,366 private elementary and secondary schools in the United States, schools defining themselves in the "other religious" category represented the highest percentage, with 46.8 percent. Secular private schools made up 31.9 percent of nonpublic U.S. schools, and only 21.3 percent were affiliated with the Roman Catholic Church.[17]

The decline of Catholic schools has been, in part, attributed to a "dwindling Catholic population." Michael Griffin, superintendent of diocesan schools in Fall River, Massachusetts, noted that at least 10 percent of the student population attending Catholic schools are not Catholic.[18] Though non-Catholic parochial schools have seen an attendance boost, they are not the institutions most blamed for the decline in Catholic school attendance. Chester E. Finn Jr. attributes the overall 13 percent drop in private school enrollment from 2000 to 2010 to the rising popularity of charter schools.[19] Data from the U.S. Census Bureau's 2010 population survey was analyzed by Stephanie Ewert of the Social, Economic, and Housing Statistics Division. Ewert found "a statistically significant correlation between the decline in private school enrollment and the growth of charter schools. . . . The data also reveal that private school enrollment decline was not triggered by the economic recession."[20]

Since the 2010 release of the documentary *Waiting for Superman*, which focused on several families hoping for their children's acceptance into a charter school, the public eye has been trained on the charter school phenomenon. Charter schools, though technically public, have distinctly nonpublic characteristics, not the least of which is exemption from many state educational mandates. Charter schools are begun and managed by independent founders or private businesses. These charters are good for only five years before they must be reviewed. The schools are tuition free, and students are selected on a lottery system.

Teachers in charter schools are not necessarily required to have state certification, although many schools elect to operate under a particular system, requiring teachers to have certification for their particular programs. Montessori and expeditionary learning methods are two popular charter school structures. Research about the success of charter schools has been mixed, but there has been a significant number of positive studies recently. Studies in Massachusetts demonstrated that Boston charter school students "gained an additional one and a half more months of learning per year in reading and an additional two and a half more months of learning per year in math . . . compared with their regular public school counterparts."[21]

One of the primary effects of the recent upswing in the popularity of charter schools has been renewed fervor in the debate about school choice. Politicians have remained split on the issue, as many conservatives have pushed for vouchers allowing parents to use government money to send children to private and parochial schools, a use that many Democrats claim violates the separation of church and state. Charter schools have proven themselves a middle ground as the battle rages on about the use of public money for private school vouchers.

The argument on the conservative side is that the free marketization of education would create competition, essentially forcing all schools to raise their quality to continue attracting students. Since charter schools provide choice without forcing the voucher issue, they have been quickly embraced by many states. Connecticut's House of Representatives approved a bill allowing school districts with charter schools to count the charter schools' scores on state tests as a part of their districts' average academic achievements. The Texas legislature increased its charter school cap to allow 330 by 2020.[22]

While the school choice issue has pushed itself to the forefront of educational debate, there is one contestant in the running that has grown quietly in the last twenty years. In 1992, America was home to 300,000 homeschoolers, a number that rapidly grew to more than 1 million by 1998. The spring of 2007 showed 1.5 million homeschool students. National Household Education Surveys administered in 2003 and 2007 found the following:

- Eighty-eight percent of homeschooling parents chose to home-school because of concern about the school environment—this was the primary reason for homeschool listed by 21 percent of the parents surveyed.
- Eighty-three percent wished to provide religious or moral instruction for their children—36 percent reported that this was the most important reason for their decision to homeschool.
- Seventy-three percent were dissatisfied with the academic instruction available at other schools—only 17 percent cited this as the main reason for their choice to homeschool.[23]

Although children in homeschool, charter, and private schools have been largely exempt from governmental regulations on education—a factor that has played a large role in the educations of millions of children—recent policy has begun to affect even nonpublic schools. As noted in chapter 10, the College Board has begun to revise the SAT, and it is possible that the ACT and GED will also be revised to better reflect the Common Core curriculum currently being implemented in millions of public schools across the nation. Nonpublic schools have had freedom from such mandates because of their exemption from state testing requirements. However, many private and parochial schools pride themselves on their ability to prepare students for college. As the Common Core begins to infiltrate assessments of college readiness, it is likely that nonpublic schools will need, on some level, to begin conforming to the Common Core standards.

Another major factor that will greatly affect the future of our schools and that of teaching is the influence of educational technology. Public and private schools are being encouraged to spend vast amounts of money on this initiative. This trend is the subject of our next chapter.

NOTES

1. Jack Jennings, "Proportion of U.S. Students in Private Schools is 10 Percent and Declining," *Huffington Post*, March 28, 2013, http://www.huffingtonpost.com/jack-jennings/proportion-of-us-students_b_2950948.html.

2. L. Dean Webb, Arlene Metha, and K. Forbis Jordan, *Foundations of American Education* (Upper Saddle River, NJ: Merrill, 2000), 457.

3. Pearl Rock Kane, ed., *Independent Schools, Independent Thinkers* (San Francisco: Jossey-Bass, 1992), 8–12.

4. Center for Education Reform, "K–12 Facts," http://www.edreform.com/2012/04/k-12-facts/.

5. Kane, *Independent Schools,* 8.

6. Luis Benveniste, Martin Carnoy, and Richard Rothstein, *All Else Equal, Are Public and Private Schools Different?* (New York: RoutledgeFalmer, 2003), 100.

7. Center for Education Reform, "K–12 Facts."

8. Benveniste, Carnoy, and Rothstein, *All Else Equal*, 131.

9. Benveniste, Carnoy, and Rothstein, *All Else Equal*, 131.

10. Benveniste, Carnoy, and Rothstein, *All Else Equal*, 135.

11. Kane, *Independent Schools*, 9.

12. Kane, *Independent Schools*, 9.

13. Kane, *Independent Schools*, 11.

14. "Class Size," *Education Week*, July 1, 2011, http://www.edweek.org/ew/issues/class-size/.

15. Leonard Baird, "Elite Schools: Recent Research from the Outside and from the Inside," paper presented at the annual conference of the American Educational Research Association, Washington, DC, April 1987, 3.

16. Webb, Metha, and Jordan, *Foundations of American Education*, 457.

17. U.S. Department of Education, "Statistics about Non-public Education in the United States," http://www2.ed.gov/about/offices/list/oii/nonpublic/statistics.html.

18. Michael Gagne, "Catholic Schools Optimistic through Difficulties," *Taunton Gazette*, July 20, 2013, http://www.tauntongazette.com/news/x1676638240/Catholic-schools-optimistic-through-difficulties?zc_p=0.

19. Katie Ash, "Are Small Private Schools a Dying Breed?" *Education Week*, May 24, 2013, http://blogs.edweek.org/edweek/charterschoice/2013/05/are_small_private_schools_a_dying_breed.html?qs=parochial+schools.

20. Katie Ash, "Exploring the Link between Charters and Private School Enrollment Decline," *Education Week*, April 9, 2013, http://blogs.edweek.org/edweek/charterschoice/2013/04/census_bureau_researcher_explores_link_between_charters_and_private_school_enrollment_decline.html.

21. Katie Ash, "Massachusetts Charters Outperform Regular Schools, Study Finds," *Education Week*, February 28, 2013, http://blogs.edweek.org/edweek/charterschoice/2013/02/boston_charters_see_significant_learning_gains_credo_says.html?qs=charter+schools.

22. Katie Ash, "This Week's Roundup of School Choice News," *Education Week*, April 26, 2013, http://blogs.edweek.org/edweek/charterschoice/2013/04/this_weeks_roundup_of_school_choice_news.html?qs=school+choice.

23. U.S. Department of Education, "Statistics about Non-public Education."

III

Future

FOURTEEN

The Influence of Technology

In any speculative conversation about the future of education, technology is undoubtedly a major topic. Already, colleges and even high schools across the country are offering online degrees; elementary schools are making use of tablets; and the Internet is rapidly becoming a focus of research courses. It is unfair to argue that such developments are entirely bad, just as it is unfair to argue that they are entirely good. What we can do is observe the trends and changes related to technology in our classrooms and speculate about where it may take us.

Essentially, technology is pervading our classrooms in two major ways: as a means for education and as a topic for education. Perhaps no development has had as major an impact on the modern educational climate than the Internet. In her book *Net Curriculum*, Linda Jones poses questions related to that first goal: "How can we successfully integrate the resources available on the Internet into classrooms or library media centers? What strategies can we use with students to help them become better navigators and informed consumers? What skills do our students need to effectively utilize the Internet?"[1]

Many teachers and administrators are still wrestling with these questions years after the arrival of the Internet as a resource. In many ways, our schools are in flux. The methods and goals of the classrooms in which many of us grew up are no longer relevant to a generation with a wealth of information constantly at its fingertips. The question we must ask is this: How are classrooms keeping up, and which methods for integrating technology and education can be considered effective?

One major way that schools are becoming more technologically relevant is through the integration of new technologies into the classroom. Interactive SMART Boards, personal laptops, and tablets are all making appearances in the average classroom and enjoying success where they are implemented correctly. Unfortunately, however, there are many obstacles preventing total victory for technology in schools.

For one, Internet speeds in many schools are just too slow to be worthwhile. E-rate, a 1996 initiative to bring connectivity to schools and libraries, provides low-cost Internet connections to community institutions, although the speeds of those services are rarely much different from those of home subscribers, at about 20 megabits per second. Such speeds are more than adequate for the average home consumer but cause slow operation in schools where dozens of classrooms are trying to view video or listen to audio files simultaneously.[2]

There does seem to be some hope for faster speeds in the near future. On a visit to a North Carolina middle school in June 2013, the president called on the Federal Communications Commission to expand the E-rate program. The update will provide schools with Internet speeds of up to 1 gigabit per second and allow schools to pay for wireless networks throughout their buildings and campuses.[3]

Another hindrance to the effective use of technology in classrooms is the self-control that it requires from students and community members. In an *Education News* article, Muhammad Nadeem highlighted the enormous theft problem that many districts face. He holds up the Cleveland Heights–University Heights School District, which provided thirteen hundred iPads to its middle school students as an example. "Less than a week after the district handed out the tablets, the district saw more than a dozen students had been mugged on the way home from school. The thieves had learned to deactivate a tracking software on the tablets so they stole iPads exclusively."[4] Already, districts are responding to these challenges. For example, Coachella Valley Unified issued iPads equipped with security systems that can be removed only by Apple itself and will shut down automatically unless they "check in" with the district before connecting to the Internet.[5]

Light-fingered community members do not present the only threat to effective use of technology in the classroom. Another *Education News* article written by Nadeem outlined the results of a study indicating that most students use digital devices for non-class-related purposes. The study focused solely on college and university students and found that more than 90 percent of students at six institutions used their digital devices for noneducational activities during class time. Still, the students reported advantages to using their devices in class. "The top three cited were staying connected (70%), avoiding boredom (55%), and doing related classwork (49%)."[6]

The rapid adoption of new technologies is also a cause for concern among some experts. In her article "Are Schools Embracing Cheap Technology Too Quickly?" Julia Lawrence explains, "Because the price of consumer technology like personal use electronic tablets have fallen in recent years, many schools used the opportunity to purchase a large number of such gadgets for students to use in aid of learning. However, questions are now being asked if the education establishment is not moving too fast and too soon to digitize their classrooms, and if some vital parts of learning aren't being lost in the bright glitter of an iPad screen."[7] She quotes Patrick Gray, a writer for TechRepublic, who argues that digitization might not be a complete solution:

> Despite being the beneficiary of technology at school, I'm not sold on the concept of equipping every student with a tablet, allowing Wikipedia to be used as a primary source, and YouTube videos of underwater life substituting for another high point of my elementary school career: donning rubber boots and netting tadpoles and water bugs under the auspices of science. Tablets and technology, in general, seem as if they should be an accelerator for competent instruction. However, in the United States, they're too often employed as a replacement for it.[8]

Gray himself is able to recognize the potential for argument, however, wondering, "If perhaps there were someone like me three decades ago, lamenting the invasion—in meticulous handwritten cursive, of course—of noble institutions of learning by Apples, Commodores, Tandys, and the occasional IBM PC. I would have scoffed at this curmudgeon who felt I could learn logic without the crutch of GW-BASIC."[9]

Certainly, there is an argument to be made for the use of these technological advancements in the modern classroom. As Gray observed, the old technologies that we left behind seem incredibly outdated, and there is a real possibility that future students will think the same about books, paper, and pencils. In fact, for many of us, the advantages of computer use already seem apparent, especially when we consider the accomplishments of students who come from homes with computers compared to those of students without. One study conducted for Germany's Centre for Economic Studies IFO contradicted that commonplace in May 2013.

The study chose more than a thousand students without computers in grades 6–10, in fifteen Californian schools and provided half those students with free computers. The results would probably be classified as "surprising" by many Americans. "We find no evidence that treatment students spent more or less time on homework, and we find that the computers had no effect on turning homework in on time, software use, computer knowledge, and other intermediate inputs in education."[10]

Although no conclusive results have shown whether technology use is inherently beneficial to student learning, it can safely be argued that technology is only as effective as the teacher implementing it. As Tracy Gray, a managing director for the American Institutes for Research, wisely suggested, "technology is like putting a piano in the room and expecting everybody to be Chopin. Unless teachers know how to use the technology and the students have the necessary support they need to master the course content, then it can only go so far."[11]

There is little use in pretending that some schools have not had success in implementing major technological changes. In the Netherlands, seven "Steve JobsSchools" opened in 2013, where students each receive their own iPads "to offer highly customized lessons tailored to teach individual child's learning speed, style, and skill."[12] According to Christina Chaey, teachers at these schools "act more like 'coaches' rather than conveyors of knowledge."[13] She cites Dutch entrepreneur and initiator of Education for a New World, Maurice De Hond, who asserted, "A child starting school today has to be prepared for the world of 2030 and after, a world even more digitized than today's world. But most schools are preparing their students for yesterday's world."[14]

To support the use of iPads as replacement instructors, the schools claim that the nature of virtual learning allows education to happen at 24/7, 365 days a year, giving parents and children more flexibility to have important life experiences without falling behind academically.

Online education programs like those appearing in the Netherlands are also making their way to American high schools. Articles in *Education News* and *ABC Newspapers* highlighted the stories of Atlanta Virtual Academy and StepAhead, two online schools in Georgia and Minnesota, respectively. The Atlanta Virtual Academy program was introduced to improve on the 51 percent graduate rate for Atlanta public schools. Students are required to log on between twenty and twenty-four hours a week for summer classes and for twelve to fifteen hours a week during the regular school year. Since July 2012, Georgian students have had the opportunity to choose between free state-provided online courses and their local districts.[15]

Alternatively, some students have opted to combine traditional instruction with online classes. Kjarra Wymore, a student at Blaine High School, chose not to enroll in StepAhead, a full-time online high school, instead opting to take online courses in an à la carte manner:

> "You have the forums online, but that's not, generally speaking, getting to know your classmates," she said. Still, she appreciates the online option. If she was just starting high school, she would consider taking language and history classes online, but not science classes—they are too hands-on, Wymore said. For her health class, it was convenient to work at her own pace, she said. Additionally, she found that she needed to be very self-motivated, which will serve her well in college where she will need that same drive, according to Wymore.[16]

In an acknowledgment that online schools are not for everybody, StepAhead offers this minisurvey on its website to help students assess whether online high school is the right option for them:

1. Do you struggle with the rigidness of the typical school day?
2. Are you comfortable with technology?

3. Do you like to learn at your own pace—whether that's faster or slower than others?
4. Are you proficient in reading?
5. Do you prefer to study at different times every day?
6. Are you self-disciplined and organized?
7. Would you like to arrange your classes to suit your schedule? [17]

Despite attempts like these to attract only prepared, dedicated, and self-aware students, online K–12 schools have not achieved the high results that many have hoped for. Julia Lawrence noted in one article, "Students in online schools substantially underperform their peers in traditional schools. The results are particularly dismal in math, writing, and science, although. . . . The readying achievement levels among the students are nothing much to write home about either." [18]

Despite less-than-stellar results, support for online education seems to be growing. A Gallup poll conducted in October 2013 found that a full third of Americans feel that online schools are equal to traditional schools. Still, many reported that they felt it provides "less rigorous testing and grading and less qualified instructors than traditional, classroom-based education."

It is no surprise that Americans have mixed opinions about online education and technology in the classroom—Americans seem to have mixed opinions about almost everything. Still, it merits examination that technology is continuing to dominate the classroom, despite ongoing debate. Success does not appear to be consistent, even though certain studies have indicated positive trends related to technology in the classroom. One study found that 20 percent more students scored *proficient* or *advanced* in subject comprehension for Algebra 1 when using tablets rather than their paper-based textbook counterparts. [19]

The question of technology in the classroom is one that is fiercely debated by educators, not because it poses a question of art versus science, but because, in many ways, it threatens the profession of teaching as we know it. There is, undoubtedly, less chance for teachers to directly interact with their students and therefore less of a chance for teachers to have personal impacts on their students. For multitudes of teachers, the draw to the teaching profession lies in the ability to form relationships with students and to help them discover their strengths, talents, values, and future selves.

The advent of the digital classroom brings with it plenty of uncertainty about the future of the teaching profession. The only thing that does seem certain is that education is once again on the cusp of a major shift. Digital technology stands poised to change the face of teaching much in the same way that the printing press revolutionized schools of the Renaissance and public schools forever changed the trajectory of American education.

While nobody seems able to predict the changes that technology will bring to American education, many are increasingly relying on educational research to reveal important information about what effective teaching looks like. This imprecise intersection of science and teaching has gathered quite a following across the United States and is the subject of our next chapter.

NOTES

1. Linda C. Joseph, *Net Curriculum: An Educator's Guide to Using the Internet* (Medford, NJ: Information Today, 1999), xv.

2. Jackie Calmes and Edward Watt, "Obama Promises to Have High-Speed Internet in Most Schools in 5 Years," *New York Times*, June 6, 2013, http://www.nytimes.com/2013/06/07/us/politics/obama-to-seek-more-internet-aid-for-schools.html.

3. Calmes and Watt, "Obama Promises."

4. Muhammad Nadeem, "School-Issued iPads, Laptops Become Target for Thieves," *Education News*, November 12, 2013, http://www.educationnews.org/technology/school-issued-ipads-laptops-become-target-for-thieves.html.

5. Nadeem, "School-Issued iPads."

6. Muhammad Nadeem, "Most Students Use Digital Devices for Non-class Purposes," *Education News*, October 29, 2013, http://www.educationnews.org/technology/study-most-students-use-digital-devices-for-non-class-purposes.html.

7. Julia Lawrence, "Are Schools Embracing Cheap Technology Too Quickly?" *Education News*, May 28, 2013, http://www.educationnews.org/technology/are-schools-embracing-cheap-technology-too-quickly.html.

8. Lawrence, "Are Schools Embracing?"

9. Lawrence, "Are Schools Embracing?"

10. Richard Chirgwin, "Computer Use Irrelevant to Education Outcomes, Says US Study," *Register*, May 21, 2013, http://www.theregister.co.uk/2013/05/21/computer_ownership_schools_study/.

11. Muhammad Nadeem, "Georgia Schools Using Online Education to Improve Graduation Rate," *Education News*, August 12, 2013, http://www.educationnews.org/online-schools/atlanta-schools-using-online-education-to-improve-graduation-rate.html.

12. Christina Chaey, "In the Netherlands, Schools Are Letting iPads Do the Teaching," http://www.fastcompany.com/3016125/fast-feed/in-the-netherlands-schools-are-letting-ipads-do-the-teaching?partner=rss.

13. Chaey, "In the Netherlands."

14. Chaey, "In the Netherlands."

15. Chaey, "In the Netherlands."

16. "Anoka-Hennepin Unveils Full-Time Online High School," *ABC Newspapers*, October 15, 2013, http://abcnewspapers.com/2013/10/15/anoka-hennepin-unvels-full-time-online-high-school.

17. "Anoka-Hennepin Unveils Full-Time."

18. Julia Lawrence, "Online Schools' Underwhelming Results Could Threaten Industry," *Education Week*, October 4, 2013, http://www.educationnews.org/online-schools/online-schools-underwhelming-results-could-threaten-industry.html.

19. Christina Bonningon, "iPad a Solid Education Tool, Study Reports," *Gadget Lab*, January 20, 2012, http://www.wired.com/gadgetlab/2012/01/ipad-educational-aid-study/.

FIFTEEN

The Impact of Educational Research

A topic as seemingly nebulous as educational research seems almost impossible to address in its entirety in only one chapter. However, educational research stands at the center of nearly every educational innovation with which teachers have been presented, especially in the current climate of scientific pedagogy. To begin, it seems prudent to specifically identify what is meant by the term *educational research*. Educational research is not so different from research in the field of natural science. A theory—that is, a carefully considered set of ideas about a particular pedagogical method—is developed and then tested on groups of real learners in an attempt to either prove or disprove the theory. Educational implications of a proven theory are then considered before researchers determine the best practice for implementation.[1]

But how does educational research make its way into our classrooms? Arthur K. Ellis and Jeffrey T. Fouts, authors of *Research on Educational Innovations*, offer this explanation:

> A common claim of most educational innovations is that they are "research-based." The intent, apparently, is to give school personnel cause to think that a particular program is valid and reasonable for them to use because it will yield improved results. The term *research-based* lends almost mystical qualities to the innovations, making it difficult if not impossible for the average teacher, administrator, or school board member to challenge the claims made in behalf of the innovation. . . . The fact is that many school personnel simply do not understand the arcane procedures of educational research with its language of statistical analysis, control groups, experimental designs, etc. As a result, they are left to the mercy of persuasive arguments by "experts" who tell them what the research says and what they should therefore do.[2]

Today's teachers are not strangers to this scenario. No Child Left Behind mandated that schools spend their grant funds on evidence-based strategies, effectively making research a nonnegotiable presence in American schools.

It is not our aim to create an image of villainous researchers twisting their moustaches as they develop theories about how best to undermine American education. However, it does seem prudent to present an argument that counterbalances the one currently dominating the educational landscape, which evokes impressions of logical and steady white-coated researchers attempting to reason with emotionally driven, eccentric teachers. The truth is that educational research, though valuable, is imperfect.

Here we look at the facets of educational research that prevent it from being infallible, including availability of funding for educational research and implementation of research results. In addition, we discuss some real-life examples of educational research outcomes on which we currently base our educational policies.

In 2013, the Department of Education's Institute of Education Sciences, founded in 2002, was allotted an annual budget of $621.1 million.[3] Although that may sound significant, it pales in comparison to the budget allocations for other governmental agencies. In 2014, the following budgets were proposed for other departments:

Defense: $526.6 billion
Health and Human Services: $80.1 billion
Energy: $28.4 billion
Commerce: $8.6 billion
Agriculture: $22.6 billion
Veterans Affairs: $63.5 billion
Transportation: $76.6 billion
Interior: $11.7 billion[4]

Although the funding made available to the Institute of Education Services is already paltry in comparison with that offered to other departments, the expectations imposed on the educational sector are no less rigorous. Despite the appearance of such articles as "White House Hastens Research Results" in *Education Week* and other periodicals, many are questioning the usefulness of research produced under rigorous constraints and limited budgets.

In her *Education Week* article "Lawmakers Question Education Research's Usefulness," Sarah D. Sparks noted, "Federal education research has gotten more scientifically rigorous, but in a time of shrinking agency budgets, Congress is debating whether it is practically useful." She pointed to the testimony heard on September 10, 2013, from top researchers interested in improving the Institute of Education Sciences. Representative John Kline explained, "As we develop policies to strengthen the institute, we should consider streamlining the federal research structure to reduce duplication, enhance accountability, and make it easier for states and school districts to access important information."[5]

The consensus seemed to be that research, though more rigorous than ever before, was not really being utilized effectively. In another article, Sparks described the major obstacles to implementation as presented by George A. Scott, director of the Government Accountability Office's education, workforce, and income security issues.

- "Some of IES' [Institute of Education Services'] initiatives, such as the research and development centers, do not have clearly defined audiences or ways to measure whether they are responding to their users' needs."
- "Results of research often come too late for them to be of use to policymakers or practitioners. In particular, [Government Accountability Office] noted that IES' average peer review time has lengthened from 117 days in fiscal year 2011 to 175 days in fiscal year 2012."
- "IES does not routinely translate all of its research into language easy for non-academics to understand."[6]

Interviews with state education officials seem to confirm the office's findings. A 2010 and 2011 study of the research use and practices of three states found that the following were given the most credence in all three states: studies generated in-house and advice from colleagues. Sparks explained in a third article, "Even though policymakers and program officers in the states were open to research, they also said they need considerably more support from so-called 'knowledge brokers,' who can boil down research findings and translate them for the specific state's context."[7]

Sparks went on to provide a possible explanation as expressed by Carrie Conaway—Massachusetts associate education commissioner for planning, research, and delivery systems—who lamented that researchers rarely took the extra step of making sure their findings are relevant and usable. As a result, Conaway and other state education officials were found to be far more likely to use research evaluating programs and interventions than they were raw data. Conaway herself affirmed, "Implementation studies would have saved us a lot of time reinventing the wheel."[8]

Authors of a Boston College study agreed. "There's too much being written and not much being done. These reports are like stones in a lake; you get a big plop and then it fizzles out," said Henry I. Braun. His study hoped to get legislators thinking about new approaches with model legislative language. One of his associates, Jamie Horwitz, agreed: "Increasingly what NEPC is trying to do is not just underwriting research on an area of education or problem of education, but also a legislative solution. We want to provide concrete ways to make a fix."[9]

Although some officials have expressed greater interest in evaluation of programs and implementation than in raw data, there are certainly those of differing opinions. Nancy Flanagan emphasized another point of view in her reflection "My Research Is Better Than Your Experience." Flanagan argues that policy implications are the least defensible parts of any research paper and that they tend to reflect the inherent biases of researchers. "It's remarkable," she avers, "how many well-done research studies present credible evidence, then go off on an implications bender. Even when evidence is shaded or questionable or very limited, the boldness of the associated policy recommendations would often make your head spin, if you were a practitioner, that is, thinking about how this would play out in an actual school."[10]

Flanagan referred to an article in *Scientific American* that explored the issue of learning styles in instruction and asked whether it was a "bogus idea." She noticed that psychologists, professors, and a pediatric optometrist contributed to the discussion, each vying to prove that his or her research was most truthful, and she asked the question, "Notice anybody missing in this discussion?"[11]

Flanagan also cites a blog post by Sarah Darer Littman, who presented her personal experience implementing learning styles in the classroom. "What informs my teaching most is parenting a child who thinks, processes, and learns very differently than I do," explained Littman. Flanagan agrees, concluding, "That's the sticking point in utilizing research findings to make grand pronouncements about how schools should operate, or how teachers should teach. We leave out the most important voice, that of the actual people doing the actual work, and the ideas they find useful."[12]

What seems to have developed in the field of educational research is a tension between researchers and teachers, both of whom feel that they hold the more important puzzle piece, essentially personifying the art-versus-science debate. Inasmuch as educators such as Flanagan and Littman speak for the art side, Gina Kolata takes the podium for science in her *New York Times* article "Guesses and Hype Give Way to Data in Study of Education." Kolata champions the work of the What Works Clearinghouse, which she describes as a "mini Food and Drug Administration, but without enforcement power—that rates evidence behind various programs and textbooks, using the same sort of criteria researchers use to assess effectiveness of medical treatments."[13]

Her parallels to the world of medicine are echoed by Grover J. Whitehurst of the Brookings Institution, who likens a lack of randomized clinical trials in education to failing medical professionals. "It's as if the medical profession worried about the administration of hospitals and patient insurance but paid no attention to the treatments that doctors gave their patients," he insists. Going on, he describes the status of education research as "poor" when he was appointed as the director of the Institute of Education Sciences in 2002. "It was far more humanistic and qualitative than crunching numbers and evaluating the impact. You could pick up an education journal and read pieces that reflected on the human condition and that involved interpretations by the authors on what was going on in schools. It was more like the work a historian might do than what a social scientist might do." [14]

While education researchers focus on the data and numbers informing classroom decision making, many teachers are concerned about what those data overlook. Jack Schneider takes this position in "What's Missing from Education Policy Debate." A former teacher himself, he explains,

> What policy elites don't talk about—what they may not even *know* about, having themselves so little collective teaching experience—is how much relationships matter in our nation's classrooms. Yes it matters that history teachers know history and chemistry teachers know chemistry. But it also matters that history teachers know their students, and that chemistry teachers know how to spot a kid in need. It matters that teachers have strong academic backgrounds. But it also matters that they can relate to young people—that they see them, hear them, and care for them. [15]

Despite the ongoing debate between proponents of scientific data and proponents of artistic pedagogy, study after study has gone through the Institute of Education Sciences, and many have contributed to major policy changes in districts across the country. One example is the decision of many schools to lengthen their school days or school years. One article shared the story of a New Orleans school that chose to start school in mid-July, and the author closed with this interesting observation: "The jury's still out on whether more time adds up to more learning. A 2012 literature review by the nonprofit research center Child Trends found most schools that added time showed academic growth. Yet it was impossible to attribute the improvement directly to more time in school. And the report concluded that when it comes to education, more time will never compensate for bad teaching." [16]

Whether or not additional time spent in school really affects educational success, it is interesting to note that schools are citing "research" as a reason to lengthen the school day, although research has been unable to definitively support that particular method. On the other side, many studies are touted in the media as being significant but are rarely seen sparking innovation in American schools.

A recent study published in a journal called *Education* demonstrated "that ninth graders have the lowest grade point average, the most missed classes, the majority of failing grades, and more misbehavior referrals than any other high-school grade level."[17] Diane Ravitch keenly expressed her skepticism about the study's effect:

> Many schools allow students to advance ready or not, and when they reach the ninth the stakes are higher. The high-stakes testing starts in the tenth grade so kids are being held back not for their own sake but to protect their school's statistics. If the focus were really on the students, people would be thinking creatively about how to help them instead of thinking of them as data points.[18]

A similar conundrum can be seen in relation to a second study finding that only about a third of thirteen thousand young children tracked from kindergarten through middle school were on track with cognitive skills by third grade. Although the data strongly suggest that school systems are failing children at a young age, the recommendations made are rather vague. Among the "several policy recommendations to address the gaps" are suggestions such as "quality birth-through-8 education programs" and "promoting communication."[19]

In many ways, it appears that those on each side of the debate are engaged in a colossal game of pedagogical tug-of-war. While champions of data and research are pulling for homogeny and clearly defined answers, proponents of anecdotal evidence and personal experience are pulling for creativity and personal connections. However, neither side seems to have stopped to consider that the other may have something to offer. Perhaps the best solution is a middle ground.

NOTES

1. Arthur K. Ellis and Jeffrey T. Fouts, *Research on Educational Innovations,* 2nd ed. (Larchmont, NY: Eye on Education, 1997), 5.

2. Ellis and Fouts, *Research on Educational Innovations*, 5.

3. U.S. Department of Education, "Fiscal Year 2011 Budget Summary," http://www2.ed.gov/about/overview/budget/budget13/justifications/x-ies.pdf.

4. "Federal Research and Development Funding: FY2014," January 18, 2014, http://www.whitehouse.gov/sites/default/files/omb/budget/.

5. Sarah D. Sparks, "Lawmakers Question Education Research's Usefulness," *Education Week,* September 18, 2013, http://www.edweek.org/ew/articles/2013/09/18/04esra_ep.h33.html?qs=research.

6. Sarah Sparks, "What Should Be the Federal Role in School Research?" *Education Week,* September 10, 2013, http://blogs.edweek.org/edweek/campaign-k-12/2013/09/what_should_be_the_federal_rol.html?qs=research.

7. Sarah D. Sparks, "Connection to Education Research Elusive for States," *Education Week,* March 22, 2013, http://blogs.edweek.org/edweek/inside-school-research/2013/03/states_seek_education_research_connection_.html?qs=research.

8. Sparks, "Connection to Education Research."

9. Sarah D. Sparks, "Scholars Call for New Approach to Data for Accountability," *Education Week,* October 23, 2013, http://blogs.edweek.org/edweek/inside-school-research/2013/10/using_data_for_accountability.html.

10. Nancy Flanagan, "My Research Is Better Than Your Experience," *Education Week,* September 24, 2013, http://blogs.edweek.org/teachers/teacher_in_a_strange_

land/2013/09/my_research_is_better_than_your_experience.html?qs=research.   Accessed 17 November 2013.

11. Flanagan, "My Research Is Better."

12. Flanagan, "My Research Is Better."

13. Gina Kolata, "Guesses and Hype Give Way to Data in Study of Education," *New York Times*, September 2, 2013, http://www.nytimes.com/2013/09/03/science/applying-new-rigor-in-studying-education.html.

14. Kolata, "Guesses and Hype."

15. Jack Scheider, quoted in Valerie Strauss, "What's Missing from Education Policy Debate," *Washington Post*, September 6, 2013, http://www.washingtonpost.com/blogs/answer-sheet/wp/2013/09/06/whats-missing-from-education-policy-debate.html.

16. Sarah Carr, "To Improve Learning, Some Schools Lengthen the School Day or Year," July 31, 2013, http://hechingerreport.org/content/to-improve-learning-some-schools-lengthen-the-school-day-or-year.html.

17. M. Nadeem, "Research Points to Ninth Grade as the Most Important High School Year," *Education News*, November 12, 2013, http://www.educationnews.org/education-policy-and-politics/research-points-to-ninth-grade-as-the-most-important-high-school-year.html.

18. Nadeem, "Research Points to Ninth Grade."

19. M. Nadeem, "Study Finds Majority of Kids Lagging in Cognitive Skills by 3rd Grade," *Education News*, November 12, 2013, http://www.educationnews.org/education-policy-and-politics/study-finds-majority-of-kds-lagging-in-cognitive-skills-by-3rd-grade.html.

SIXTEEN

Concluding Thoughts

In closing, we return to the issue that has arisen frequently during this historical survey of the teaching process. At a number of points along the way, we have raised the question of whether teaching is an art or a science. While most observers might conclude that there are elements of both art and science in the practice of teaching, it is our concern that in twenty-first-century America, this nation continues in a perilously empirical direction rather than in the view of teaching as an art form.

The current emphasis on assessment through testing is placing the results of these written examinations as the most important way of evaluating school programs. Test results are currently being used as a major factor in evaluating teachers and principals, and they are utilized in judging the effectiveness of our school programs.

There is little doubt that this trend is causing teachers to "teach to the test." Subjects other than those tested are being de-emphasized in other schools. Music, art, and physical education have seen class time reduced, especially in urban schools where there is the most concern about low test scores. Coupled with the primary importance being given to tests is the fact that some teachers are being forced to utilize scripted lessons, during which they follow the teacher's manual almost word for word. In some schools, teachers at a grade level are put on a structured daily schedule that assigns a specific time limit for every lesson and mandates that teachers stay with the grade-level calendar.

Another concern that we have mentioned is the growing trend to create schools that are totally online. It is our fear that this approach to teaching makes almost impossible the kind of personal impact that a teacher can have on his or her students. Some online programs, those called *hybrid*, do maintain limited personal contact between student and instructor. The research shows that students are more comfortable and complimentary of this approach than of those classes that are totally online. There is also the opportunity of using video technology to at least allow face-to-face interaction within a class. Still, one cannot help but question whether the science that makes all this possible is limiting the personal impact that teachers have had through the ages.

An additional trend that some critics suggest is limiting the flexibility of teachers in their own classrooms is the movement toward the national Common Core curriculum. Many teachers are worried about taking time for field trips, projects, and innovative lessons. In search of a way to improve test scores, we appear to be reducing teachers' freedom to innovate. Some skeptics have raised the question of whether our current commitment to extensive testing is another attempt at using scientific methods in our teaching. Those concerned with these changes see our current primary objective in American education as the improvement of our test scores compared to those of other countries. Others have expressed worries that the excessive attention to tests will reduce the personal impact that teachers have on their students.

For two decades, students in one introductory course at Roberts Wesleyan College have written essays about teachers who have influenced them the most. Almost none of these essays have mentioned tests. Instead, students talk about how the teacher had created in them a love of a subject, and they often mentioned the exciting and innovative methods that the teacher used. Perhaps even more important is the fact that these teachers provided influential role models for their students. They demonstrated not only a love for the subject they taught but also a sincere concern for their students.

The great teachers in Western history did not rely on scientifically tested teaching manuals nor Common Core curricula. Instead, they combined a love of their subjects and a true concern for their students, causing them to have lifelong impacts on those whom they taught. As we attempt to improve our schools, it is important that we not forget those lessons that great teachers have taught us.

History's greatest educators were also not at the mercy of teams of educational researchers. As research continues to dominate the decision-making process, we would do well to remember that there is no "best answer" for every classroom. In fact, efforts to find a singular pathway to success for all students are quite futile. Indeed, it is only the well-practiced, artful teacher who can connect on a personal level with his or her pupils, fueling their interest in learning, confidence in their capabilities, and, ultimately, academic growth.

As research begins to erode the personal connections that teachers have with their students and to resist the involvement of educators in the decision-making process, technology has emerged not as a tool for learning but as a replacement for teachers. As long as this is allowed to continue, the American school system is liable to continue its rapid trek toward the impersonalization of learning, the disappearance of inspired teaching, and the elimination of the heart and soul of education. No more will students be able to reminisce about particular teachers who helped them unlock their potentials, identify their strengths, and surmount challenges. Character education will lose its luster, and many students will lose the opportunity to identify positive role models.

While research and technology are not, by themselves, bad or wrong, our extreme reliance on them is cause for alarm. Certainly, there must be some way to counterbalance the heart and mind in teaching, allowing both the science of pedagogy and the art of connection to coexist harmoniously. For now, however, the inexorable march toward the science and systemization of teaching seems to be persistent and inescapable.

This concern about making teaching too much of a science is not new. In 1950, Gilbert Highet, in his book *The Art of Teaching*, wrote that he chose the title because he believed that "teaching is an art, not a science." He went on to argue that, for him, it was

> very dangerous to apply the aims and methods of science to human beings as individuals, although statistical principles can often be used to explain their behavior in large groups, and a scientific diagnosis of physical structures is always valuable. But a "scientific" relationship between human beings is bound to be inadequate and perhaps, distorted. . . . Teaching involves emotions, which cannot be systematically appraised and employed, and human values, which are quite outside the grasp of science.[1]

Perhaps the best-selling author in the field of education, Jonathan Kozol, began sounding the alarm about making teaching a science in his 1981 book *On Being a Teacher*. Here, he criticized the fact that teachers were being asked to carefully follow teacher guides produced by publishers. For him, these supposedly helpful manuals were designed "to help the teacher put across the lessons without needing to devote a vast amount of time to preparation. . . . Unfortunately, while seeming to make the teacher's job more simple, the teachers' guides are also taking away the satisfaction of all independent and creative labor in the preparation of the daily work. . . . It robs the teacher of the only intellectual dignity which our profession still allows us: the individual, passionate, or whimsical exhilaration of invention."[2]

Larry Cuban, a contemporary critic of current trends, has pointed out that since Highet's book in 1950, we did see a short period in the mid-1980s until early 1990 when "a progressive movement for portfolios, project based teaching, performance based assessment, and other student centered approaches found their way into some schools." For him, this period of experimentation declined because of the pursuit of higher test scores. In his mind, it has been followed by almost a quarter century of business influence upon education "through philanthropy, partnerships, and the imitation of corporate practices."[3]

He believes that, as a result, "public schools have become more business-like in governance and management, and in offering parents choices in schools."[4] Cuban goes on to state that "the bottom line has shifted from better teaching and learning to higher test scores. Now, only one kind of 'good' district, only one kind of 'good' school, and only one kind of 'good' teaching has become politically correct."[5] An article in the *Washington Post* notes, "For decades, business leaders have been saying that they want workers who are problem solvers, flexible thinkers, and collaborators with a strong work ethic." The author goes on to raise several questions for those supporting the business model in schools:

- "Are children more likely to learn these skills if their main motivation is success on tests and their teachers are competing for merit bonuses if they and their teachers practice these skills in their learning?"
- "Do you want workers who are only driven by bonus pay or workers who are spurred to excellence by self-motivation and teamwork?"
- "Are teachers and their students more likely to learn innovation in a compliance fear-of-failure culture, or in a collaborative learning-from-failure culture."
- "Given limited resources, which is a wiser investment, new teacher evaluation systems to reward the top and fire the bottom 10% of teachers or intensive, sustained professional development and support for all current teachers?"[6]

Another individual who is writing about current trends in teaching is Henry A. Giroux. He has called for resistance to attempts "to transform pedagogy into the mere application of standardized practical methods and techniques. Otherwise, teachers become indifferent to the ethical and practical dimensions of their own authority and practice." Concerning the influence of business, he argues, "Market-driven notions of management do not mobilize the individual imagination and social vision. On the contrary, they do everything possible to make them irrelevant to the discourse of leadership."[7]

Valerie Strauss, writing for the *Washington Post*, has made the argument that there is reason for the United States to consider a moratorium on high-stakes testing. She agrees with Randi Weingarten, the leader of the American Federation of Teachers, who has said, "We aren't saying students shouldn't be assessed. . . . We aren't saying teachers shouldn't be evaluated. We're not saying that there shouldn't be standardized tests. We are talking about a moratorium on consequences in these transitional years."[8] The fact is that, as a result of federal pressure, teacher evaluations in most states are now tied, in part, to test results. This—along with the simultaneous need to adapt to the Common Core standards—has created great stress and tension for many of our teachers and principals.

If, indeed, our current trends in American education are upsetting the balance in our schools, it may be helpful to pause and remember that teachers must do more than teach to the test. Almost everyone has, in one way or another, been inspired by a teacher who has had a significant impact on his or her life. Throughout history, people with imagination, creativity, and compassion have positively affected our society. It continues to be important that we give to our teachers the flexibility in their profession to pursue goals other than test preparation. As a nation, we do need to improve teaching and our schools. Too many students and schools are failing, especially in our cities and poor rural areas. There are steps that we can take that might be worth trying.

For example, there is an increasing consensus that early childhood education can make a difference, especially in the communities where schools are failing. We can also learn from the success of other nations. Finland has proven that the development of a respected, well-paid teaching profession can also have a positive impact. We need to make teaching a profession that can draw and keep many of our best and brightest people. Perhaps like many other countries, we need to attempt to have our students spend more time in school.

Most of all, we need to reduce the gap in educational opportunity between the haves and the have-nots in our society. Presently, children living with affluent families in the suburbs attend schools financed by high property taxes, which provide programs that are not available in poorer districts. Schools and teachers alone cannot solve the opportunity gap problem. One way to move forward in reducing the differences in educational opportunity between the wealthy and the rest of the population is to find ways to reduce the opportunity gap. If this is to happen, our society has to understand the importance of what teachers do .

President John F. Kennedy stated the problem this way: "Modern cynics and skeptics see no harm in paying those to whom they entrust the minds of their children a smaller wage than is paid to those whom they entrust to care for their plumbing."[9] Paying teachers more will not in itself solve our national educational problems, but recognizing the importance of what teachers can do certainly will help. There is no question that we should continue to do research to find ways to improve what is occurring in our schools. Horace Mann was correct when he wrote, "Teaching is the most difficult of all arts, and the profoundest of all sciences. . . . Arithmetic, grammar, and the other rudiments, as they are called, comprise but a small part of the teachings in a school. The rudiments of feeling are taught not less than the rudiments of thinking."[10]

Still, as we pursue the quest for knowledge about learning and teaching, we should remember the words of John Steinbeck, who wrote, "I have come to believe that a great teacher is a great artist and that there are as few as there are any other great artists. Teaching might even be the greatest of the arts since the medium is the human mind and spirit."[11]

NOTES

1. Gilbert Highet, *The Art of Teaching* (New York: Vintage Books, 1950), 1.

2. Jonathan Kozol, *On Being a Teacher* (Oxford, UK: Oneworld, 2009), 49.

3. Kozol, *On Being a Teacher*, 17.

4. Larry Cuban, *Why Is It So Hard to Get Good Schools?* (New York: Teachers College Press, 2003), 13.

5. Cuban, *Why Is It So Hard?*

6. Valerie Strauss, "Key Questions Begging for Answers about School Reform," *Washington Post*, July 18, 2013, http://www.washingtonpost.com/blogs/answer-sheet/wp/2013/07/18/key-questions-begging-for-answers-about-school-reform/.

7. Henry A. Giroux, *Education and the Crisis of Public Values: Challenging the Assault on Teachers, Students, & Public Education* (New York: Lang, 2012), 82–96.

8. Valerie Strauss, "Why We Need a Moratorium on the High Stakes of Testing," *Washington Post*, May 15, 2013, http://www.washingtonpost.com/blogs/answer-sheet/wp/2013/05/15/why-we-need-a-moratorium-on-the-high-stakes-of-testing/.

9. Valerie Strauss, "Appreciating Teachers (for a Change)," *Washington Post*, May 9, 2013, http://www.washingtonpost.com/blogs/answer-sheet/wp/2013/05/09/appreciating-teachers-for-a-change/.

10. Charles M. Wiltse, *Expansion and Reform: 1815–1850* (New York: Free Press, 1967), 163.

11. Strauss, "Appreciating Teachers (for a Change)."

Index

About the Authors

Bill Hayes has been a high school social studies teacher, department chair, assistant principal, and high school principal. From 1973 to 1994, he served as superintendent of schools for the Byron-Bergen Central School District, located eighteen miles west of Rochester, New York. During his career, he was an active member of the New York State Council of Superintendents and the author of a council publication entitled *The Superintendency: Thoughts for New Superintendents*, which is used to prepare new superintendents in New York State. Mr. Hayes has also written a number of articles for various educational journals. After retiring from the superintendency, he served as chair of the Teacher Education Division at Roberts Wesleyan College in Rochester, New York, until 2003. He currently remains a full-time teacher at Roberts Wesleyan. During the past twelve years, he has written fourteen books. They include *Real-Life Case Studies for School Administrators, Real-Life Case Studies for Teachers, So You Want to Be a Superintendent?, So You Want to Be a School Board Member?, Real-Life Case Studies for School Board Members, So You Want to Become a College Professor?, So You Want to Become a Principal?, Are We Still a Nation at Risk Two Decades Later?, Horace Mann's Vision of the Public Schools: Is It Still Relevant?, The Progressive Education Movement: Is It Still a Factor in Today's Schools?, All New Real-Life Case Studies for Administrators, No Child Left Behind Past Present and Future, All New Real-Life Case Studies for Teachers,* and *What's Ahead in Education: An Analysis of the Policies of the Obama Administration, Consensus: Education Reform Is Possible.*

Alyssa Magee Lowery, a 2012 graduate of the childhood and special education program at Roberts Wesleyan College, first began her work with Mr. Hayes when she performed research for, proofread, and typed the manuscript for his last book, *Consensus: Education Reform Is Possible.* Her work on this book began when she was teaching her own classroom of four-year-olds at a private school in Rochester, New York. Currently, she is teaching preschool at another private child care institution in Rochester with goals to continue teaching, perhaps on the college level, and writing prolifically. Alyssa resides in the city of Rochester with her husband, Joshua, and enjoys exercising, cooking, crafting, and reading.

CPSIA information can be obtained at www.ICGtesting.com
Printed in the USA
BVOW05s1022230714

360167BV00001B/4/P